Finance for Non-finance Executives

Finance for Non-finance Executives

Anurag Singal

BEP BUSINESS EXPERT PRESS

First published in 2020 by
Business Expert Press, LLC
222 East 46th Street, New York, NY 10017
www.businessexpertpress.com

ISBN-13: 978-1-95253-832-2 (paperback)
ISBN-13: 978-1-95253-833-9 (e-book)

Business Expert Press Finance and Financial Management Collection

Collection ISSN: 2331-0049 (print)
Collection ISSN: 2331-0057 (electronic)

Cover image licensed by Ingram Image, StockPhotoSecrets.com
Cover and interior design by S4Carlisle Publishing Services Private Ltd., Chennai, India

First edition: 2020

10 9 8 7 6 5 4 3 2 1

Printed in the United States of America.

Abstract

This book is intended to help professionals, especially from functional areas other than finance, such as sales, marketing, human resource, research and development, production, and procurement, to gain an extensive working knowledge of critical financial principles in an easy-to-follow manner, enabling them to make critical business decisions involving cost-savings, budgets, new projects decisions, growth strategies, and so on.

This book introduces you to the key concepts of finance so you can contribute to the success of your business. It will help you understand the language used by accountants and how financial statements fit together. Furthermore, you will understand how to use ratio analysis to get a sense of the company's performance. In addition, you will learn the concepts of management accounting and various kinds of decisions, including make-or-buy, shutdown, and so on. You will gain an understanding of how to implement Budgeting and Working Capital Management. The exciting part is also the chapter on Investment Appraisal, where you will learn how to evaluate business proposals from a return standpoint.

Keywords

finance for non-finance executives; finance for dummies; financial statements; financial accounting; management accounting; investment appraisal; decision making; costing

Contents

CHAPTER 1

Financial Statements

Why Accounting Matters for Non-financial Professionals?

Ironically, while money drives us all, a lot of laymen are alienated from financial knowledge not because of intelligence but because of fear.

It is imperative to understand the subject and language of finance if managers are to communicate with authority within a business. After all, finance is the language used in the boardroom.

Accounting is best left to accountants, right? Actually, that's not true. All non-financial professionals stand to benefit from a firm grasp of basic accounting concepts. Being able to back up your business proposals, projects, and ideas with numbers puts you in a stronger position, as does being able to recognize the financial value of your work—how you contribute to the bottom line.

- Can we just do without looking at the financial portion?
- Only if the world operates without money!

Learning to Read Financial Statements

Suppose a friend came to you and asked you to invest in her new business. She has started a website design business and would like more money to buy a new computer. Before you decide if you should invest in her business or not, think about the questions you would want to ask her. What questions did you come up with? Here are a few you might have thought of:

- How much cash does the company already have?
- How much revenue has the company made since it was started? In the past year?

- How much revenue does the company expect to make in the future?
- What has the company spent its cash on in the past?
- Does the company have any debt?

In order to answer these questions, a good place to start would be to look at the company's financial statements. Learning to read financial statements is like learning a new language.

If you want to order a good dish in a French restaurant, you will need to speak French to read the menu. Similarly, with companies, if you want to find a good stock to invest in, you will need to speak the language of finance and read their financial statements. Just like learning any new language, it is difficult at first, but the more you practice, the more fluent you will become!

At the most basic level, financial statements give you information that is predominantly quantitative
- How much it sells and at what cost
- How much cash it generates
- How many assets it has and whether these are owned by banks or shareholders

However, they also provide insight into
- Who owns it and who are the major stakeholders
- How it is organized and who are the key decision makers
- Market share/growth targets
- Level of concern for its employees/community
- What the chairman looks like (!)

So some qualitative data is provided.

And if you look really hard and read between the lines, they may provide
- A window into the company's strategy
- Economics of the industry/competitors

Financial Statements Provide Information about Firms' Economic Activities

These range from raising funds from investors to running the business operations to generate profit, which is either reinvested in the business or distributed to the investors in the form of dividend (Figure 1).

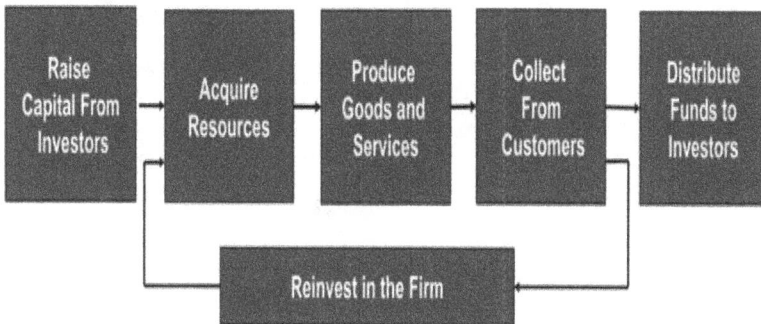

Figure 1

Definition of Accounting

- Accounting is a system for recording information about business transactions and events.
- Accounting systems slice the firm's life into arbitrary periods (quarters and years). This allows for the generation of more timely information.
- To provide summary statements of a company's financial position and performance to users who require such information.
- There are three key components of financial statements.
- This helps get standardized reports for external stakeholders.
- A major motive is tax accounting in compliance with Internal Revenue Service (IRS) rules for computing taxes payable.
- Managerial accounting uses custom reports for internal decision making.

Role of Financial Reporting

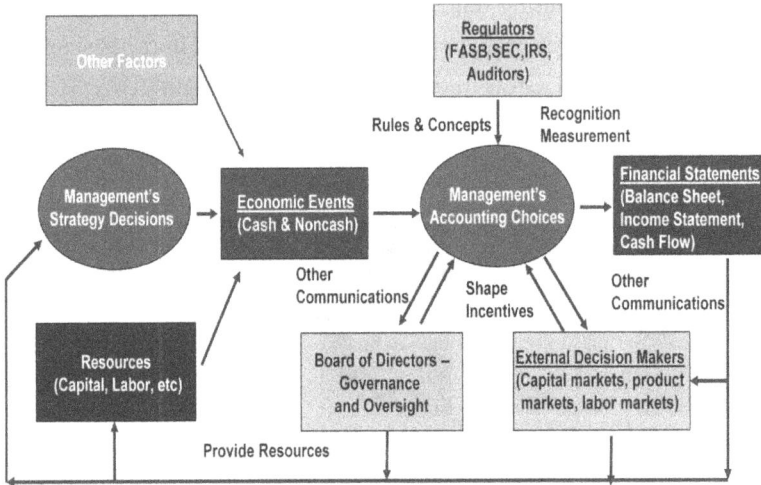

Figure 2

Financial Reporting Requirements

- Each country has its own financial reporting requirements
- In the U.S., The Securities and Exchange Commission (SEC) requires periodic financial statement filings:
- 10-K: Annual report (within 60 days for big firms)
- 10-Q: Quarterly report (within 40 days for big firms)
- 8-K: Current report (material events)
- Proxy, registration, and insider trading statements
- In other countries, firms file semiannual reports instead of quarterly reports
- Firms supplement filings with voluntary disclosure
- Conference calls, press releases, forecasts, presentations at brokerage conferences

Who Makes the Accounting Rules?

Generally Accepted Accounting Principles (GAAP) are established by U.S. Congress, but they delegate to the SEC, which in turn delegates to the Financial Accounting Standards Board (FASB).

International Financial Reporting Standards (IFRS) are required in over 100 countries, including the EU.

The two sets of rules are increasingly similar, but are not the same. Financial Statements Provide Information about Firms' Economic Activities.

Annual Report Contents

It is a comprehensive document that discusses
- Firm's strategy, products, competitive environment
- Financial statistics
- Management discussion and analysis (MD&A)
- Financial statements
- Footnotes that explain the accounting procedures used by the firm and discuss various assumptions regarding how the numbers were calculated

What Are the Required Financial Statements?

- Balance Sheet
- Financial position (listing of resources & obligations) on a specific date
- Assets = Liabilities + Stockholders' Equity
- Income Statement
- Result of operations over a period of time
- Net income = Revenues – Expenses
- Statement of Cash Flows
- Sources and uses of cash during a period of time
- Operating, Investing, and Financing Activities
- Statement of Stockholders' Equity
- Change in stockholders' equity over a period of time (Figure 3)

1. Profit And Loss Account	2. Statement Of Cash Flows	3. Balance Sheet
Matches revenues with costs • Profit: revenue > cost • Loss: revenue < cost	Shows the changes in cash • Over the accounting period	a) Lists the assets owned by the firm b) Details how these assets are financed • Shareholders (equity) • Lenders (liability)
States the results of the firm's operations • Over a period of time • Including accounting adjustments, e.g., depreciation	States actual transactions without accounting adjustments	Snapshot of firm's financial position • On the day the statement was prepared • Cumulative - represents result of all transactions that have taken place up to that point

4. Notes To The Accounts
Contain explanatory information in addition to or in respect of the above statements e.g., revenue split by geography/segment, financials of acquisitions/discontinued businesses etc.,

Figure 3

The balance sheet shows the following:

A) What does the firm own?
B) How was it paid for?

Assets = Liabilities + Owner's Equity (Figure 4)

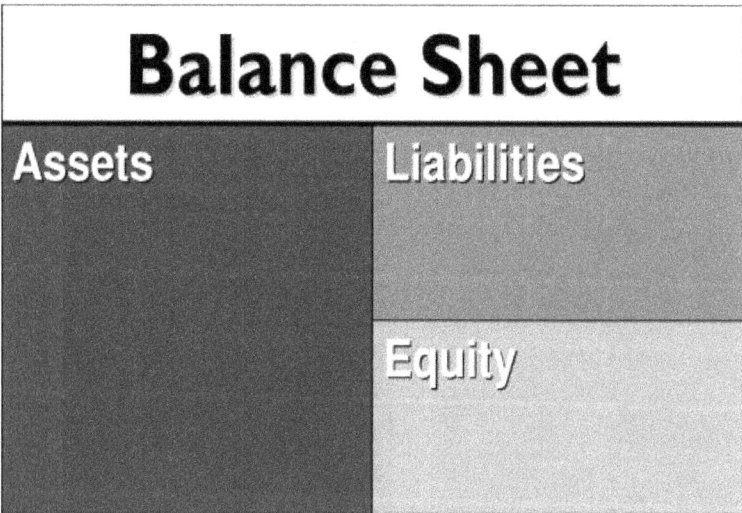

Balance Sheet

Assets

Liabilities

Equity

Figure 4

Which of the Following Are Recognized as Assets on the Balance Sheet?

- Cash ✓
- Accounts receivable ✓
- Customers' promises to buy products in the future ✗
- Prepaid insurance ✓
- Inventory ✓
- Brand name ?
- Discovery of a new medicine ✗
- Competitor goes bankrupt ✗
- Hire a new CEO ✗

Figure 5

Which of the Following Are Liabilities?

- Accounts payable ✓
- New customer signs a contract to buy product in the future ✗
- Receipt of payment in advance of providing service ✓
- Long-term debt ✓
- Product warranties ✓
- Employee pensions ✓
- Lawsuit is filed against the company ✗

Figure 6

If we were to apply this to your personal life, this can be represented diagrammatically as follows:

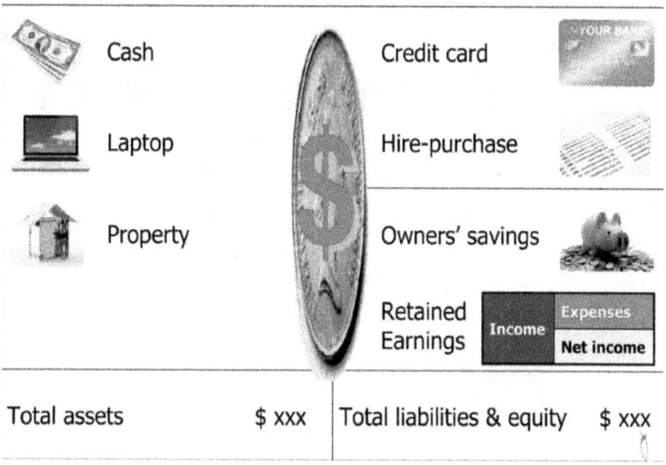

	Cash		Credit card	
	Laptop		Hire-purchase	
	Property		Owners' savings	
			Retained Earnings	Income / Expenses / Net income
Total assets	$ xxx		Total liabilities & equity	$ xxx

Figure 7

From a statutory financial statements perspective, the components are:

Current Assets

- Cash and marketable securities
- Accounts receivable
- Inventories

Property, Plant, and Equipment

- Land, buildings
- Machinery
- Accumulated depreciation

Other Assets

(E.g., Intangibles)

The Other Side

Liabilities

- Short-term (payables, current debt, etc.)
- Long-term (deferred taxes, long-term debt)

Shareholders' Equity

- Preferred and common stock (par value)
- Retained earnings

To represent it diagrammatically:

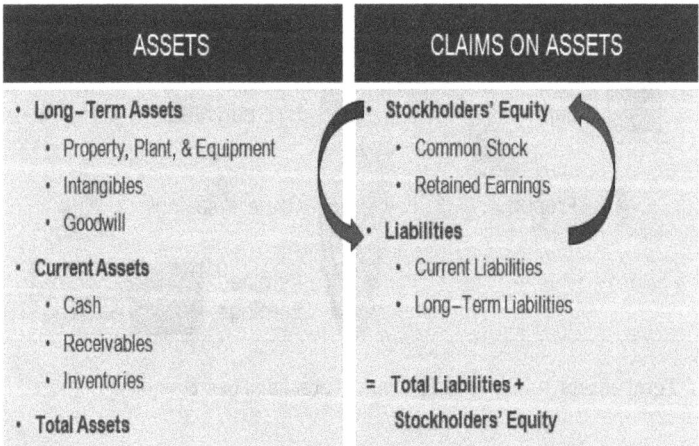

ASSETS	CLAIMS ON ASSETS
• **Long–Term Assets**	• **Stockholders' Equity**
• Property, Plant, & Equipment	• Common Stock
• Intangibles	• Retained Earnings
• Goodwill	• **Liabilities**
• **Current Assets**	• Current Liabilities
• Cash	• Long–Term Liabilities
• Receivables	
• Inventories	= **Total Liabilities +**
• **Total Assets**	**Stockholders' Equity**

Figure 8

Let us consider the financials of Google (Alphabet Inc.) from the form 10-K filed with SEC and see how the balance sheet is prepared in accordance with the statutory norms. The statement essentially depicts the sources of funds and application of the same. You can track individual line items and see the yearly change; also for ratio analysis, as we will learn later (Figure 9).

Cash and cash equivalents	$ 16,701	$ 18,498
Marketable securities	92,439	101,177
Total cash, cash equivalents, and marketable securities	109,140	119,675
Accounts receivable, net of allowance of $729 and $753	20,838	25,326
Income taxes receivable, net	355	2,166
Inventory	1,107	999
Other current assets	4,236	4,412
Total current assets	135,676	152,578
Nonmarketable investments	13,859	13,078
Deferred income taxes	737	721
Property and equipment, net	59,719	73,646
Operating lease assets	0	10,941
Intangible assets, net	2,220	1,979
Goodwill	17,888	20,624
Other noncurrent assets	2,693	2,342
Total assets	$ 232,792	$ 275,909
Liabilities and Stockholders' Equity		
Current liabilities:		
Accounts payable	$ 4,378	$ 5,561
Accrued compensation and benefits	6,839	8,495
Accrued expenses and other current liabilities	16,958	23,067
Accrued revenue share	4,592	5,916
Deferred revenue	1,784	1,908
Income taxes payable, net	69	274
Total current liabilities	34,620	45,221
Long-term debt	4,012	4,554
Deferred revenue, noncurrent	396	358
Income taxes payable, noncurrent	11,327	9,885
Deferred income taxes	1,264	1,701
Operating lease liabilities	0	10,214
Other long-term liabilities	3,545	2,534
Total liabilities	55,164	74,467
Commitments and Contingencies (Note 10)		
Stockholders' equity:		
Convertible preferred stock, $0.001 par value per share, 100,000 shares authorized; no shares issued and outstanding	0	0
Class A and Class B common stock, and Class C capital stock and additional paid-in capital, $0.001 par value per share: 15,000,000 shares authorized (Class A 9,000,000, Class B 3,000,000, Class C 3,000,000); 695,556 (Class A 299,242, Class B 46,636, Class C 349,678) and 688,335 (Class A 299,828, Class B 46,441, Class C 342,066) shares issued and outstanding	45,049	50,552
Accumulated other comprehensive loss	(2,306)	(1,232)
Retained earnings	134,885	152,122
Total stockholders' equity	177,628	201,442
Total liabilities and stockholders' equity	$ 232,792	$ 275,909

Figure 9

Income Statement (Statement of Earnings)

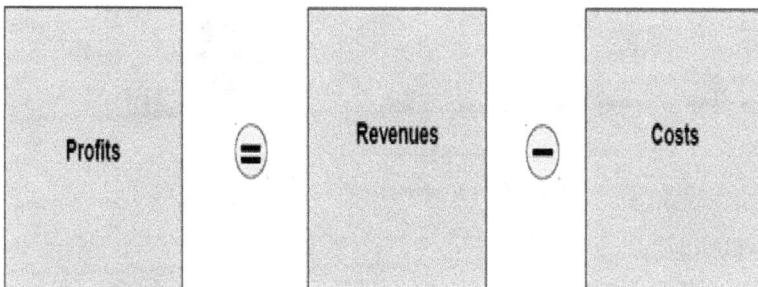

Figure 10

The sequence is:

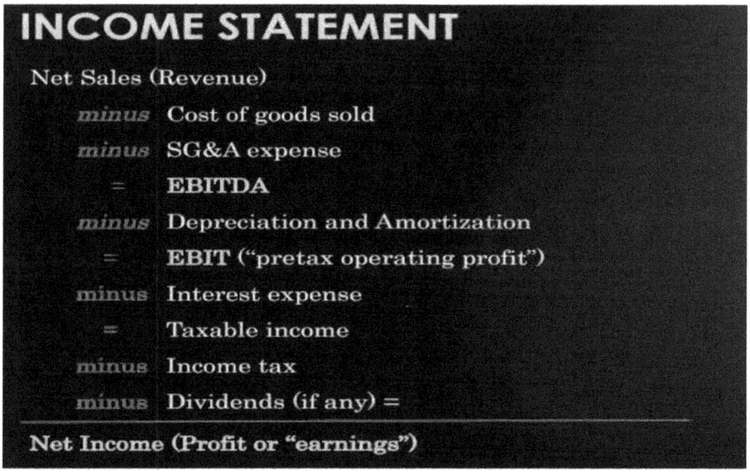

INCOME STATEMENT

Net Sales (Revenue)

 minus Cost of goods sold

 minus SG&A expense

 = EBITDA

 minus Depreciation and Amortization

 = EBIT ("pretax operating profit")

 minus Interest expense

 = Taxable income

 minus Income tax

 minus Dividends (if any) =

Net Income (Profit or "earnings")

Figure 11

Movement in the Balance Sheet can be seen in the P&L

Alphabet Inc.
CONSOLIDATED STATEMENTS OF INCOME
(In millions, except per share amounts)

	Year Ended December 31,		
	2017	2018	2019
Revenues	$ 110,855	$ 136,819	$ 161,857
Costs and expenses:			
Cost of revenues	45,583	59,549	71,896
Research and development	16,625	21,419	26,018
Sales and marketing	12,893	16,333	18,464
General and administrative	6,840	6,923	9,551
European Commission fines	2,736	5,071	1,697
Total costs and expenses	84,677	109,295	127,626
Income from operations	26,178	27,524	34,231
Other income (expense), net	1,015	7,389	5,394
Income before income taxes	27,193	34,913	39,625
Provision for income taxes	14,531	4,177	5,282
Net income	$ 12,662	$ 30,736	$ 34,343
Basic net income per share of Class A and B common stock and Class C capital stock	$ 18.27	$ 44.22	$ 49.59
Diluted net income per share of Class A and B common stock and Class C capital stock	$ 18.00	$ 43.70	$ 49.16

Figure 12

From the foregoing, you can track the year-wise movement in Google's line items of revenue as well as expenses, how much tax the company is paying, and how much is the net profit, which eventually flows into the balance sheet (Figures 13 and 14).

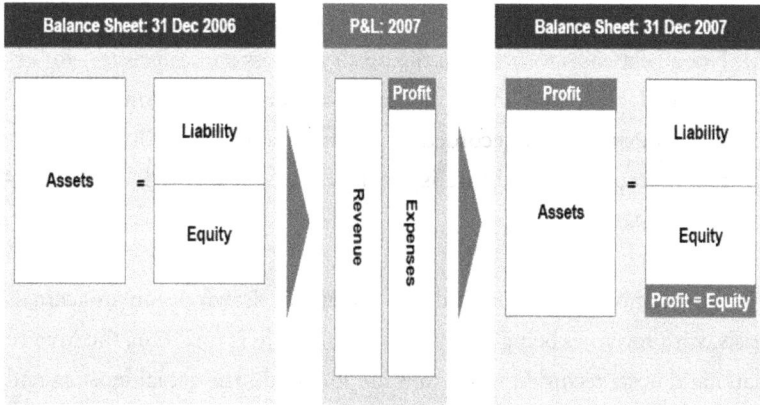

Figure 13

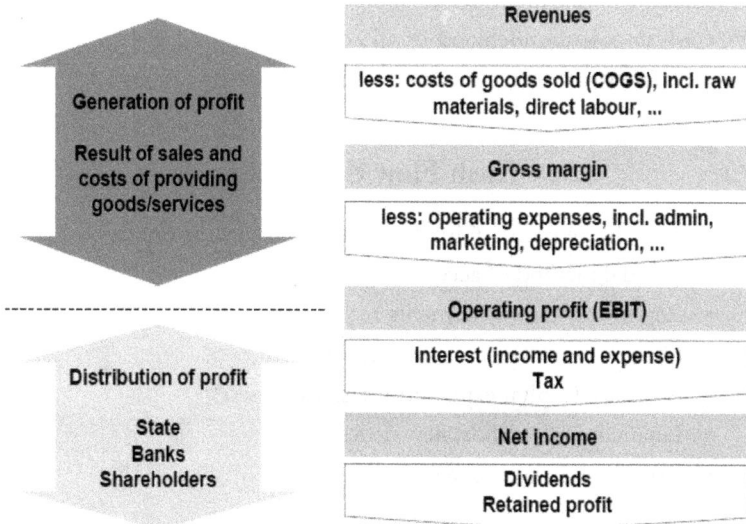

Figure 14

Cash versus Profit

Cash and profit are not the same. A loss-making company can survive as long as it has cash. A profitable company cannot survive without cash. In business, cash is king.

A profit occurs whenever revenue exceeds expenses within a period. However,

A) Not all expenses recorded in the profit and loss are cash costs—for example, depreciation and amortization of goodwill are noncash costs.
B) Not all expenses are recorded in the profit and loss account—for example, capital expenditure is recorded (i.e., capitalized) on the balance sheet.

Furthermore, the profit and loss account is drawn up on an accruals basis, with revenues being recorded when they are earned (i.e., the invoice date) and costs recorded when they are incurred. The actual receipts and payments of cash may be several weeks or months after the invoice dates, depending on the terms of business negotiated with customers and suppliers. Similarly, corporation tax for the trading period does not usually become due for payment until 9 months after the period end date.

Cash flow is the lifeblood of all companies, and it is important for every business to understand and actively manage its cash flows.

Cash Flow Statement

- Tells us the profitability during a period of time (a year)
- Accrual method of accounting
- Reports on cash movements across activities:
- Operating (net income, depreciation)
- Investing (capital expenditures, sale of assets)
- Financing (dividends, new debt)
- Reconciles balance sheet/income statement (Figure 15)

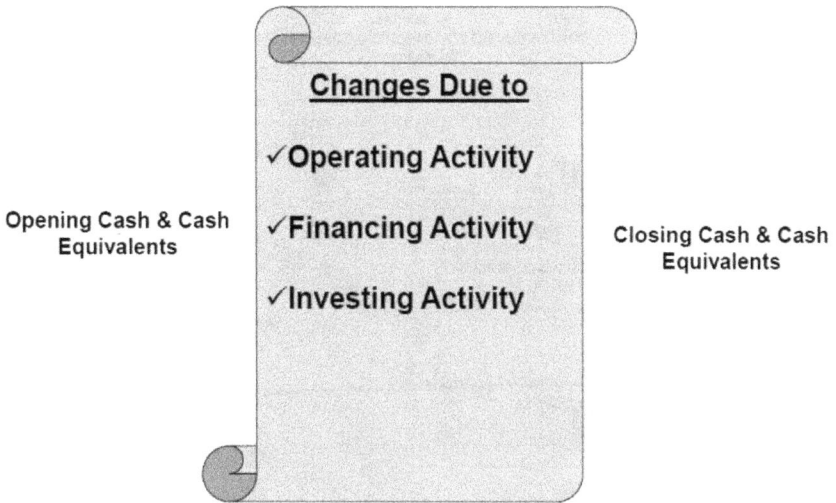

Changes Due to

✓**Operating Activity**

✓**Financing Activity**

✓**Investing Activity**

Opening Cash & Cash Equivalents

Closing Cash & Cash Equivalents

Figure 15

A company's cash flow is made up of three main constituents:

A) The cash flow from its operating activities—EBITDA less interest and taxes paid in the trading period plus the change in working capital during the trading period

B) The cash flow from its investing activities—investment in capital expenditure less the cash received from any asset disposals during the trading period

C) The cash flow from its financing activities—the change in equity and borrowings less interest and dividends paid during the trading period

Free cash flow is the cash that is free (i.e., available) to the investors who are the providers of a company's finance. Free cash flow is the cash flow from its operating activities less the cash flow from its investing activities (Figure 16).

Alphabet Inc.
CONSOLIDATED STATEMENTS OF CASH FLOWS
(In millions)

	Year Ended December 31,		
	2017	2018	2019
Operating activities			
Net income	$ 12,662	$ 30,736	$ 34,343
Adjustments:			
Depreciation and impairment of property and equipment	6,103	8,164	10,856
Amortization and impairment of intangible assets	812	871	925
Stock-based compensation expense	7,679	9,353	10,794
Deferred income taxes	258	778	173
(Gain) loss on debt and equity securities, net	37	(6,650)	(2,798)
Other	294	(189)	(592)
Changes in assets and liabilities, net of effects of acquisitions:			
Accounts receivable	(3,768)	(2,169)	(4,340)
Income taxes, net	8,211	(2,251)	(3,128)
Other assets	(2,164)	(1,207)	(621)
Accounts payable	731	1,067	428
Accrued expenses and other liabilities	4,891	8,614	7,170
Accrued revenue share	955	483	1,273
Deferred revenue	390	371	37
Net cash provided by operating activities	37,091	47,971	54,520
Investing activities			
Purchases of property and equipment	(13,184)	(25,139)	(23,548)
Purchases of marketable securities	(92,195)	(50,158)	(100,315)
Maturities and sales of marketable securities	73,959	48,507	97,825
Purchases of non-marketable investments	(1,745)	(2,073)	(1,932)
Maturities and sales of non-marketable investments	533	1,752	405
Acquisitions, net of cash acquired, and purchases of intangible assets	(287)	(1,491)	(2,515)
Proceeds from collection of notes receivable	1,419	0	0
Other investing activities	99	98	589
Net cash used in investing activities	(31,401)	(28,504)	(29,491)
Financing activities			
Net payments related to stock-based award activities	(4,166)	(4,993)	(4,765)
Repurchases of capital stock	(4,846)	(9,075)	(18,396)
Proceeds from issuance of debt, net of costs	4,291	6,766	317
Repayments of debt	(4,377)	(6,827)	(585)
Proceeds from sale of interest in consolidated entities	800	950	220
Net cash used in financing activities	(8,298)	(13,179)	(23,209)
Effect of exchange rate changes on cash and cash equivalents	405	(302)	(23)
Net increase (decrease) in cash and cash equivalents	(2,203)	5,986	1,797
Cash and cash equivalents at beginning of period	12,918	10,715	16,701
Cash and cash equivalents at end of period	$ 10,715	$ 16,701	$ 18,498

Figure 16

What to Look for in a Cash Flow Statement?

Timing of Key Events

The cash flow statement is the only financial statement that provides a clear picture of when cash actually enters or exits the business.

For projections, a key measure is often when a company or project becomes cash flow positive.

Mix of Sources and Uses of Cash

Provides insight into how a company operates:
>   —How does the company finance capacity expansions?
>   —What are the major cash drains on the company?

Ability to Cover Costs

Measures like cash flow interest coverage are useful here

Value of the Company

Many analysts will value a company on the basis of the net present value of its cash flows

Illustration

Starbucks Corp. Consolidated Income Statement

US$ in thousands

12 months ended	Sep 29, 2019	Sep 30, 2018	Oct 1, 2017	Oct 2, 2016	Sep 27, 2015	Sep 28, 2014
Company-operated stores	2,15,44,400	1,96,90,300	1,76,50,700	1,68,44,100	1,51,97,300	1,29,77,900
Licensed stores	28,75,000	26,52,200	23,55,000	21,54,200	18,61,900	15,88,600
Other	20,89,200	23,77,000	23,81,100	23,17,600	21,03,500	18,81,300
Net revenues	2,65,08,600	2,47,19,500	2,23,86,800	2,13,15,900	1,91,62,700	1,64,47,800
Cost of sales including occupancy costs	(85,26,900)	(1,01,74,500)	(90,38,200)	(85,11,100)	(77,87,500)	(68,58,800)
Gross profit	1,79,81,700	1,45,45,000	1,33,48,600	1,28,04,800	1,13,75,200	95,89,000
Store operating expenses	(1,04,93,600)	(71,93,200)	(64,93,300)	(60,64,300)	(54,11,100)	(46,38,200)
Other operating expenses	(3,71,000)	(5,39,300)	(5,53,800)	(5,45,400)	(5,22,400)	(4,57,300)
Depreciation and amortization expenses	(13,77,300)	(12,47,000)	(10,11,400)	(9,80,800)	(8,93,900)	(7,09,600)
General and administrative expenses	(18,24,100)	(17,59,000)	(13,93,300)	(13,60,600)	(11,96,700)	(9,91,300)
Restructuring and impairments	(1,35,800)	(2,24,400)	(1,53,500)	—	—	—
Litigation credit	—	—	—	—	—	20,200
Income from equity investees	2,98,000	3,01,200	3,91,400	3,18,200	2,49,900	2,68,300
Operating income	40,77,900	38,83,300	41,34,700	41,71,900	36,01,000	30,81,100
Gain resulting from acquisition of joint venture	—	13,76,400	—	—	3,90,600	—
Net gain resulting from divestiture of certain operations	6,22,800	4,99,200	93,500	5,400	—	—
Loss on extinguishment of debt	—	—	—	—	(61,100)	—
Interest income and other, net	96,500	1,91,400	1,81,800	1,02,600	43,000	1,42,700
Interest expense	(3,31,000)	(1,70,300)	(92,500)	(81,300)	(70,500)	(64,100)
Earnings before income taxes	44,66,200	57,80,000	43,17,500	41,98,600	39,03,000	31,59,700
Income tax expense	(8,71,600)	(12,62,000)	(14,32,600)	(13,79,700)	(11,43,700)	(10,92,000)
Net earnings including noncontrolling interests	35,94,600	45,18,000	28,84,900	28,18,900	27,59,300	20,67,700
Net (earnings) loss attributable to noncontrolling interests	4,600	300	(200)	(1,200)	(1,900)	400
Net earnings attributable to Starbucks	35,99,200	45,18,300	28,84,700	28,17,700	27,57,400	20,68,100

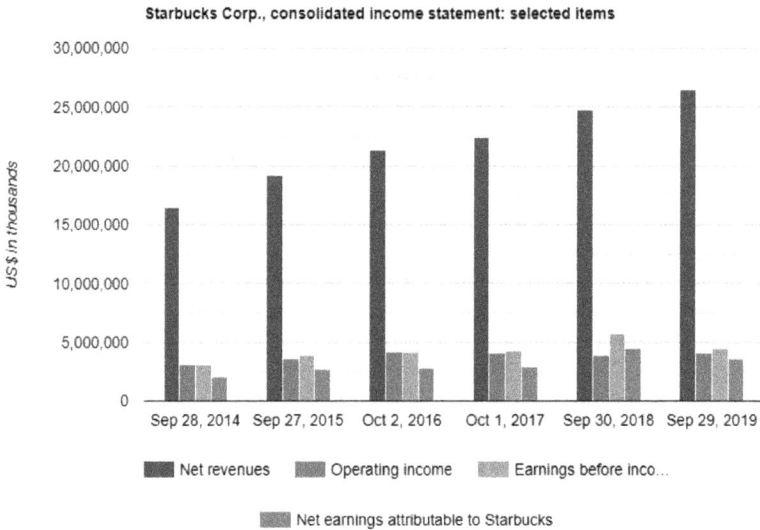

Starbucks Corp., consolidated income statement: selected items

Figure 17

Starbucks Corp.

Consolidated Balance Sheet: Assets

	Sep 29, 2019	Sep 30, 2018	Oct 1, 2017	Oct 2, 2016	Sep 27, 2015	Sep 28, 2014
Cash and cash equivalents	26,86,600	87,56,300	24,62,300	21,28,800	15,30,100	17,08,400
Short-term investments	70,500	1,81,500	2,28,600	1,34,400	81,300	1,35,400
Accounts receivable, net	8,79,200	6,93,100	8,70,400	7,68,800	7,19,000	6,31,000
Inventories	15,29,400	14,00,500	13,64,000	13,78,500	13,06,400	10,90,900
Income tax receivable	1,41,100	9,55,400	68,000	—	—	
Other prepaid expenses and current assets	3,47,100	5,07,400	2,90,100	3,50,000	3,34,200	2,85,600
Prepaid expenses and current assets	**4,88,200**	**14,62,800**	**3,58,100**	**3,50,000**	**3,34,200**	**2,85,600**
Deferred income taxes, net	—	—	—		3,81,700	3,17,400
Current assets	**56,53,900**	**1,24,94,200**	**52,83,400**	**47,60,500**	**43,52,700**	**41,68,700**
Long-term investments	2,20,000	2,67,700	5,42,300	11,41,700	3,12,500	3,18,400
Equity method investments	3,36,100	2,96,000	4,32,800	3,05,700	3,06,400	4,69,300
Other investments	59,900	38,700	48,800	48,800	45,600	45,600

Equity investments	3,96,000	3,34,700	4,81,600	3,54,500	3,52,000	5,14,900
Property, plant and equipment, net	64,31,700	59,29,100	49,19,500	45,33,800	40,88,300	35,19,000
Deferred income taxes, net	17,65,800	1,34,700	7,95,400	8,85,400	8,28,900	9,03,300
Other long-term assets	4,79,600	4,12,200	3,62,800	4,17,700	4,15,900	1,98,900
Other intangible assets	7,81,800	10,42,200	4,41,400	5,16,300	5,20,400	2,73,500
Goodwill	34,90,800	35,41,600	15,39,200	17,19,600	15,75,400	8,56,200
Long-term assets	1,35,65,700	1,16,62,200	90,82,200	95,69,000	80,93,400	65,84,200
Total assets	1,92,19,600	2,41,56,400	1,43,65,600	1,43,29,500	1,24,46,100	1,07,52,900

Income statement item	Description	The company
Net revenues	Amount, including tax collected from customer, of revenue from satisfaction of performance obligation by transferring promised good or service to customer. Tax collected from customer is tax assessed by governmental authority that is both imposed on and concurrent with specific revenue-producing transaction, including, but not limited to, sales, use, value-added and excise.	Starbucks Corp.'s net revenues increased from 2017 to 2018 and from 2018 to 2019.
Operating income	The net result for the period of deducting operating expenses from operating revenues.	Starbucks Corp.'s operating income decreased from 2017 to 2018 but then increased from 2018 to 2019 not reaching 2017 level.
Earnings before income taxes	Amount of income (loss) from continuing operations, including income (loss) from equity method investments, before deduction of income tax expense (benefit), and income (loss) attributable to noncontrolling interest.	Starbucks Corp.'s earnings before income taxes increased from 2017 to 2018 but then slightly decreased from 2018 to 2019 not reaching 2017 level.
Net earnings attributable to Starbucks	The portion of profit or loss for the period, net of income taxes, which is attributable to the parent.	Starbucks Corp.'s net earnings attributable to Starbucks increased from 2017 to 2018 but then slightly decreased from 2018 to 2019 not reaching 2017 level.

Starbucks Corp., Consolidated Balance Sheet: Assets

US$ in thousands

	Sep 29, 2019	Sep 30, 2018	Oct 1, 2017	Oct 2, 2016	Sep 27, 2015	Sep 28, 2014
Cash and cash equivalents	26,86,600	87,56,300	24,62,300	21,28,800	15,30,100	17,08,400
Short-term investments	70,500	1,81,500	2,28,600	1,34,400	81,300	1,35,400
Accounts receivable, net	8,79,200	6,93,100	8,70,400	7,68,800	7,19,000	6,31,000
Inventories	15,29,400	14,00,500	13,64,000	13,78,500	13,06,400	10,90,900
Income tax receivable	1,41,100	9,55,400	68,000			
Other prepaid expenses and current assets	3,47,100	5,07,400	2,90,100	3,50,000	3,34,200	2,85,600
Prepaid expenses and current assets	**4,88,200**	**14,62,800**	**3,58,100**	**3,50,000**	**3,34,200**	**2,85,600**
Deferred income taxes, net	---	---	---	---	3,81,700	3,17,400
Current assets	**56,53,900**	**1,24,94,200**	**52,83,400**	**47,60,500**	**43,52,700**	**41,68,700**
Long-term investments	2,20,000	2,67,700	5,42,300	11,41,700	3,12,500	3,18,400
Equity method investments	3,36,100	2,96,000	4,32,800	3,05,700	3,06,400	4,69,300
Other investments	59,900	38,700	48,800	48,800	45,600	45,600
Equity investments	**3,96,000**	**3,34,700**	**4,81,600**	**3,54,500**	**3,52,000**	**5,14,900**
Property, plant and equipment, net	64,31,700	59,29,100	49,19,500	45,33,800	40,88,300	35,19,000
Deferred income taxes, net	17,65,800	1,34,700	7,95,400	8,85,400	8,28,900	9,03,300
Other long-term assets	4,79,600	4,12,200	3,62,800	4,17,700	4,15,900	1,98,900
Other intangible assets	7,81,800	10,42,200	4,41,400	5,16,300	5,20,400	2,73,500
Goodwill	34,90,800	35,41,600	15,39,200	17,19,600	15,75,400	8,56,200
Long-term assets	**1,35,65,700**	**1,16,62,200**	**90,82,200**	**95,69,000**	**80,93,400**	**65,84,200**
Total assets	**1,92,19,600**	**2,41,56,400**	**1,43,65,600**	**1,43,29,500**	**1,24,46,100**	**1,07,52,900**

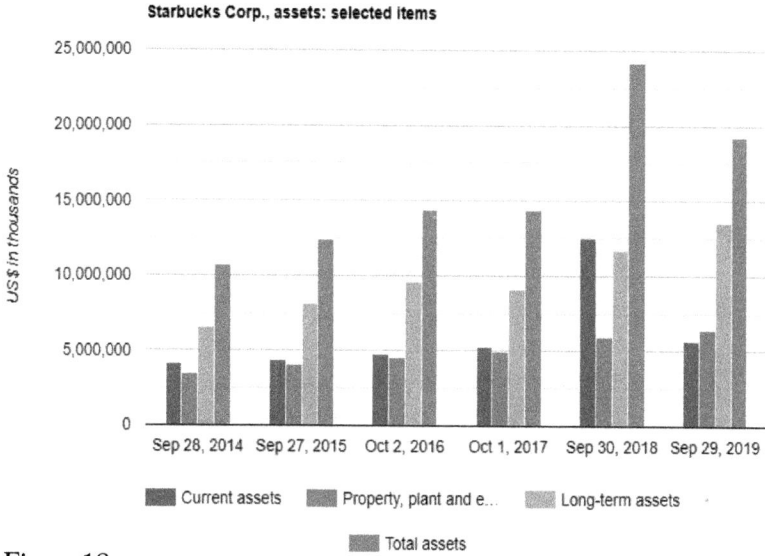

Figure 18

Balance sheet item	Description	The company
Current assets	Sum of the carrying amounts as of the balance sheet date of all assets that are expected to be realized in cash, sold, or consumed within one year (or the normal operating cycle, if longer). Assets are probable future economic benefits obtained or controlled by an entity as a result of past transactions or events.	Starbucks Corp.'s current assets increased from 2017 to 2018 but then slightly decreased from 2018 to 2019 not reaching 2017 level.
Property, plant and equipment, net	Amount after accumulated depreciation, depletion and amortization of physical assets used in the normal conduct of business to produce goods and services and not intended for resale. Examples include, but are not limited to, land, buildings, machinery and equipment, office equipment, and furniture and fixtures.	Starbucks Corp.'s property, plant and equipment, net increased from 2017 to 2018 and from 2018 to 2019.
Long-term assets	Sum of the carrying amounts as of the balance sheet date of all assets that are expected to be realized in cash, sold or consumed after one year or beyond the normal operating cycle, if longer.	Starbucks Corp.'s long-term assets increased from 2017 to 2018 and from 2018 to 2019.
Total assets	Sum of the carrying amounts as of the balance sheet date of all assets that are recognized. Assets are probable future economic benefits obtained or controlled by an entity as a result of past transactions or events.	Starbucks Corp.'s total assets increased from 2017 to 2018 but then slightly decreased from 2018 to 2019 not reaching 2017 level.

Balance sheet item	Description	The company
Cash and cash equivalents	Amount of currency on hand as well as demand deposits with banks or financial institutions. Includes other kinds of accounts that have the general characteristics of demand deposits. Also includes short-term, highly liquid investments that are both readily convertible to known amounts of cash and so near their maturity that they present insignificant risk of changes in value because of changes in interest rates. Excludes cash and cash equivalents within disposal group and discontinued operation.	Starbucks Corp.'s cash and cash equivalents increased from 2017 to 2018 but then slightly decreased from 2018 to 2019 not reaching 2017 level.
Short-term investments	Amount of investments including trading securities, available-for-sale securities, held-to-maturity securities, and short-term investments classified as other and current.	Starbucks Corp.'s short-term investments decreased from 2017 to 2018 and from 2018 to 2019.
Accounts receivable, net	Amount due from customers or clients, within one year of the balance sheet date (or the normal operating cycle, whichever is longer), for goods or services (including trade receivables) that have been delivered or sold in the normal course of business, reduced to the estimated net realizable fair value by an allowance established by the entity of the amount it deems uncertain of collection.	Starbucks Corp.'s accounts receivable, net decreased from 2017 to 2018 but then increased from 2018 to 2019 exceeding 2017 level.
Inventories	Amount after valuation and LIFO reserves of inventory expected to be sold, or consumed within one year or operating cycle, if longer.	Starbucks Corp.'s inventories increased from 2017 to 2018 and from 2018 to 2019.

Balance Sheet: Liabilities and Stockholders' Equity

	Sep 29, 2019	Sep 30, 2018	Oct 1, 2017	Oct 2, 2016	Sep 27, 2015	Sep 28, 2014
Accounts payable	11,89,700	11,79,300	7,82,500	7,30,600	6,84,200	5,33,700
Accrued occupancy costs	1,76,900	1,64,200	1,51,300	1,37,500	1,37,200	1,19,800
Accrued dividends payable	4,85,700	4,45,400	4,29,500	3,65,100	2,97,000	2,39,800
Accrued capital and other operating expenditures	7,03,900	7,45,400	6,02,600	6,17,300	5,45,200	4,44,900
Self insurance reserves	2,10,500	2,13,700	2,15,200	2,46,000	2,24,800	1,96,100
Accrued business taxes	1,76,700	1,83,800	2,26,600	3,68,400	2,59,000	2,72,000
Accrued liabilities	**17,53,700**	**17,52,500**	**16,25,200**	**17,34,300**	**14,63,200**	**12,72,600**
Accrued payroll and benefits	6,64,600	6,56,800	5,24,500	5,10,800	5,22,300	4,37,900
Income taxes payable	12,91,700	1,02,800	—	—	—	—
Stored value card liability and current portion of deferred revenue	12,69,000	16,42,900	12,88,500	11,71,200	9,83,800	7,94,500
Current portion of long-term debt	—	3,49,900	—	4,00,000	—	—
Current liabilities	**61,68,700**	**56,84,200**	**42,20,700**	**45,46,900**	**36,53,500**	**30,38,700**
Long-term debt, excluding current portion	1,11,67,000	90,90,200	39,32,600	32,02,200	23,47,500	20,48,300
Deferred revenue	67,44,400	67,75,700	4,400	—	—	—
Other long-term liabilities	13,70,500	14,30,500	7,50,900	6,89,700	6,25,300	3,92,200
Long-term liabilities	**1,92,81,900**	**1,72,96,400**	**46,87,900**	**38,91,900**	**29,72,800**	**24,40,500**
Total liabilities	**2,54,50,600**	**2,29,80,600**	**89,08,600**	**84,38,800**	**66,26,300**	**54,79,200**
Common stock; $0.001 par value	1,200	1,300	1,400	1,500	1,500	700
Additional paid-in capital	41,100	41,100	41,100	41,100	41,100	39,400
Retained earnings (deficit)	(57,71,200)	14,57,400	55,63,200	59,49,800	59,74,800	52,06,600
Accumulated other comprehensive income (loss)	(5,03,300)	(3,30,300)	(1,55,600)	(1,08,400)	(1,99,400)	25,300
Shareholders' equity (deficit)	**(62,32,200)**	**11,69,500**	**54,50,100**	**58,84,000**	**58,18,000**	**52,72,000**
Noncontrolling interests	1,200	6,300	6,900	6,700	1,800	1,700
Total equity (deficit)	**(62,31,000)**	**11,75,800**	**54,57,000**	**58,90,700**	**58,19,800**	**52,73,700**
Total liabilities and equity (deficit)	**1,92,19,600**	**2,41,56,400**	**1,43,65,600**	**1,43,29,500**	**1,24,46,100**	**1,07,52,900**

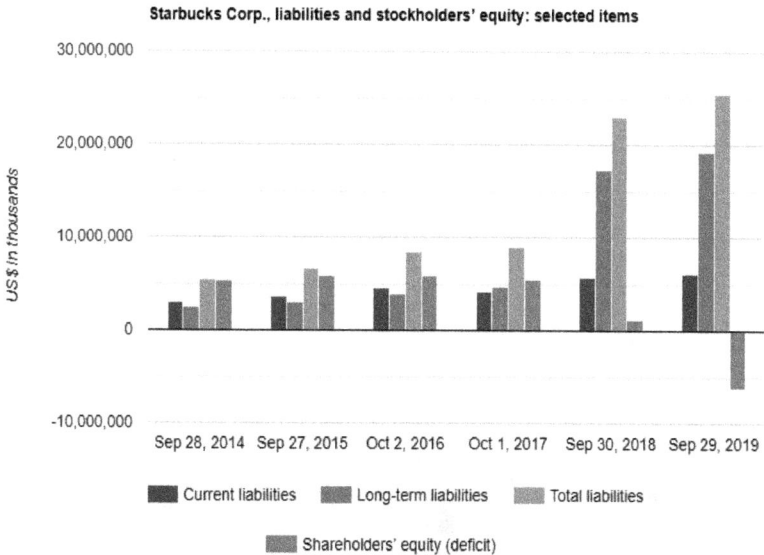

Starbucks Corp., liabilities and stockholders' equity: selected items

Figure 19

Balance sheet item	Description	The company
Current liabilities	Total obligations incurred as part of normal operations that are expected to be paid during the following twelve months or within one business cycle, if longer.	Starbucks Corp.'s current liabilities increased from 2017 to 2018 and from 2018 to 2019.
Long-term liabilities	Amount of obligation due after one year or beyond the normal operating cycle, if longer.	Starbucks Corp.'s long-term liabilities increased from 2017 to 2018 and from 2018 to 2019.
Total liabilities	Sum of the carrying amounts as of the balance sheet date of all liabilities that are recognized. Liabilities are probable future sacrifices of economic benefits arising from present obligations of an entity to transfer assets or provide services to other entities in the future.	Starbucks Corp.'s total liabilities increased from 2017 to 2018 and from 2018 to 2019.
Shareholders' equity (deficit)	Total of all stockholders' equity (deficit) items, net of receivables from officers, directors, owners, and affiliates of the entity which are attributable to the parent. The amount of the economic entity's stockholders' equity attributable to the parent excludes the amount of stockholders' equity which is allocable to that ownership interest in subsidiary equity which is not attributable to the parent (noncontrolling interest, minority interest). This excludes temporary equity and is sometimes called permanent equity.	Starbucks Corp.'s shareholders' equity (deficit) decreased from 2017 to 2018 and from 2018 to 2019.

CHAPTER 2

Analysis of Financial Statements

The Goals of Financial Analysis

Now we know that a typical Income Statement and Balance Sheet looks like this:

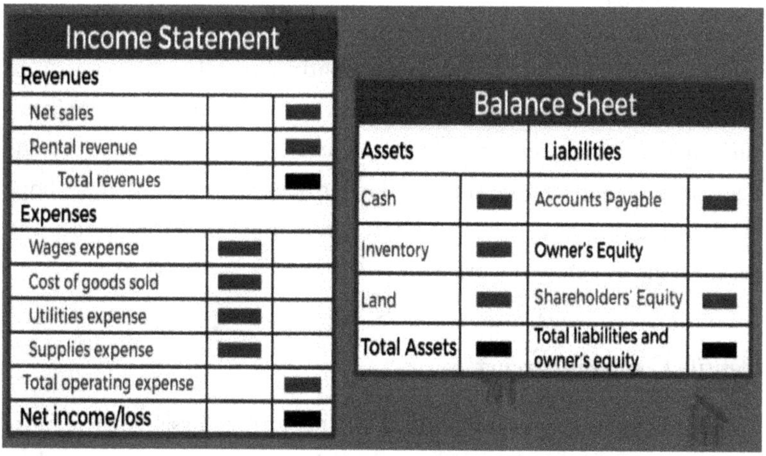

Income Statement				Balance Sheet			
Revenues							
Net sales		▬		**Assets**		**Liabilities**	
Rental revenue		▬					
Total revenues		▬		Cash	▬	Accounts Payable	▬
Expenses							
Wages expense	▬			Inventory	▬	Owner's Equity	
Cost of goods sold	▬						
Utilities expense	▬			Land	▬	Shareholders' Equity	▬
Supplies expense	▬			**Total Assets**	▬	**Total liabilities and owner's equity**	▬
Total operating expense		▬					
Net income/loss		▬					

Figure 20

Exactly what can we hope to accomplish by analyzing the financial aspects of a firm?

With the help of financial analysis, we can take investment and management decisions. Sometimes, answers will not be very clear. But we will get a lot of red flags. Both insiders and outsiders have a common goal of attempting to identify the strengths and weaknesses of the firm. While external stakeholders can also conduct a similar financial analysis, the exercise will be more robust for managers, also referred to as insiders. This is because they have access to a lot more information that is unavailable to others in the market. So when the ratios raise the "red flags," we get the answers. For example, suppose a firm discovers it has a falling profit margin. It has also found that its inventory is not selling as quickly as in the past. Insiders can order an analysis to determine which specific items are not moving well. Outsiders may only speculate about the quality of the inventory mix.

Identify Company Weaknesses

One goal of financial analysis is to identify problems that affect the firm. By identifying problems early, managers can make corrections to improve firm performance. Some problems may be hard to identify. A firm that seems to be earning profits but is constantly short of cash may turn to financial analysis to identify why this is occurring. Investors are also interested in identifying companies with problems as early as possible. No one wants to stay on a sinking ship any longer than necessary. Analysts hope they can identify firms with problems before other investors so they can sell their shares before the price drops.

Identify Company Strengths

Another equally important purpose of financial analysis is to identify company strengths so those strengths can be enhanced and used to their greatest potential. For example, in the early 1970s, falling inventory turnover ratios and return on equity ratios told JCPenney that it was unable to compete successfully with high-volume discount stores; however, it was able to sell good-quality clothing. This discovery led to a major refocusing of the firm that involved discontinuing its automotive, appliance, and furniture departments and up-scaling its clothing lines. Because of these changes, it succeeded where many of its competitors failed.

What to Look for in a P&L

Alphabet Inc.
CONSOLIDATED STATEMENTS OF INCOME
(In millions, except per share amounts)

	Year Ended December 31,		
	2017	2018	2019
Revenues	$ 110,855	$ 136,819	$ 161,857
Costs and expenses:			
Cost of revenues	45,583	59,549	71,896
Research and development	16,625	21,419	26,018
Sales and marketing	12,893	16,333	18,464
General and administrative	6,840	6,923	9,551
European Commission fines	2,736	5,071	1,697
Total costs and expenses	84,677	109,295	127,626
Income from operations	26,178	27,524	34,231
Other income (expense), net	1,015	7,389	5,394
Income before income taxes	27,193	34,913	39,625
Provision for income taxes	14,531	4,177	5,282
Net income	$ 12,662	$ 30,736	$ 34,343
Basic net income per share of Class A and B common stock and Class C capital stock	$ 18.27	$ 44.22	$ 49.59
Diluted net income per share of Class A and B common stock and Class C capital stock	$ 18.00	$ 43.70	$ 49.16

Figure 20

This Allows Year-to-Year Comparison in Performance
- Revenues are increasing
- Earnings are positive, but growth is up and down

Trends

By comparing one year with the next, it is possible to tell
- Whether a company is growing or contracting
- Whether or not it has improved efficiency
- How it may do in the future, based on qualitative or extrapolated values

Trends may also provide insight into
- Changes in supply or demand
- The competitive environment
- The broader economy

Discontinuities

These can draw your attention to areas where the company was making changes or decisions. This focus can aid in understanding

- What a company's operating strategy is
- How competitors, suppliers, or customer's behavior has affected the company

Cost and Margin

Looking at individual line items, it is possible to gain insight into the cost and margin structure of a company

- What is the breakdown between fixed and variable costs?
- How much overhead does the company carry?
- What is its operating margin?
- Does it have high interest expenses?

Margin Analysis (Common-Size Income Statement)

Common-size income statement analysis states every line item on the income statement as a percentage of sales. If you have more than 1 year of financial data, you can compare income statements to see your financial progress. This type of analysis will let you see how revenues and the spending on different types of expenses change from one year to the next.

Steps

A) Take the income statement and divide everything by that year's Sales Revenue.
B) This gives each expense item as a percentage of revenue.
C) It helps reveal the structure of your costs.
D) It tells you how each dollar of sales gets "eaten up" by different kinds of costs and how much is left over for profits.

Trying to compare data from companies that differed in size used to be an absolute nightmare. Luckily for us, vertical analysis became our savior. Just as in horizontal analysis, all of the amounts are converted into percentages. The difference lies in what pieces of data are set as 100 percent.

Vertical Analysis

In vertical analysis, the items given base values of 100 percent are the most important pieces of financial data. Everything else gets converted to percentages of those items.

Size by itself isn't an issue anymore. And the relative composition of assets, total liabilities, and equity; and revenues and expenses is revealed. Both income statements and balance sheets can be analyzed in this way.

Depending on the source document, the percentage figures result in the output of a common-size balance sheet or common-size income statement.

For a vertical analysis of a balance sheet, total assets are set as the base value, and every other asset is expressed as a percentage of it. The total liabilities and equity amount is also assigned 100 percent, and each liability and shareholders' equity account is expressed as a percentage. In the income statement, net sales is the base value having 100 percent.

The vertical analysis of a balance sheet shows how assets, liabilities, and equity are related. For example,

A) What mix of assets generates income?
B) What mix is from financing? Whether by liabilities or by equity?
C) What percentage of total assets is inventory? What happens if that percentage changes significantly?
D) What mix of various expenses has a company incurred?
E) What percentage of total assets is made up of equity? What percentage is from liabilities? And what percentage of total assets comes from accounts receivable?

Vertical analysis calculations let you examine the composition of each of the elements on a financial statement. For an income statement, it reveals how many cents of each sales dollar are absorbed by various expenses. For example, if expenses in a company equal 57.3 percent of total net sales, it means that for every $1 in sales earned, more than 57 cents goes to the costs of goods sold.

The vertical analysis of multiple years of financial statements can help you determine whether significant changes have occurred. Similarly, you can also compare between financial statement items in companies of different sizes. The first step is to transform a given year's balance sheet amounts into percentages of total assets and total liabilities. When the calculations are complete for all years, the sum of the percentages for the individual asset accounts needs to equal 100 percent. Then, because assets equal total liabilities plus equity, the sum of the percentages for the various liability and equity accounts will also equal 100 percent. It's more meaningful when the percentages are compared with competitors' or industry averages—or over a longer period of time for one company.

Using vertical analysis, you can make certain financial comparisons between companies, regardless of size or dollar amounts.

Illustration

Let us consider the example of X-Site Inc. and convert the company's income statement into a common-sized statement.

Xsite Inc Company

Consolidated Statements of Earnings

Amounts in millions except per share amounts. Years ended June 30	2xx3	2xx2	2xx1
NET SALES	$ 84,167	$ 83,680	$ 81,104
Cost of products sold	42,428	42,391	39,859
Selling, general and administrative expense	26,950	26,421	25,750
Goodwill and indefinite-lived intangible asset impairment charges	308	1,576	—
OPERATING INCOME	14,481	13,292	15,495
Interest expense	667	769	831
Interest income	87	77	62
Other non-operating income, net	942	185	271
EARNINGS FROM CONTINUING OPERATIONS BEFORE INCOME TAXES	14,843	12,785	14,997
Income taxes on continuing operations	3,441	3,468	3,299
NET EARNINGS FROM CONTINUING OPERATIONS	11,402	9,317	11,698
NET EARNINGS FROM DISCONTINUED OPERATIONS	—	1,587	229
NET EARNINGS	11,402	10,904	11,927
Less: Net earnings attributable to noncontrolling interests	90	148	130
NET EARNINGS ATTRIBUTABLE TO XSITE	$ 11,312	$ 10,756	$ 11,797

Xsite Inc.
Consolidated Statement of Earnings

	2xx3	2xx2	2xx1
Net Sales	100.0%	100.0%	100.0%
Cost of Products Sold	50.4%	50.7%	48.5%
Selling, general, and administrative expense	32.0%	31.6%	31.1%
Goodwill and indefinite-lived asset impairment	0.4%	1.9%	0.0%
OPERATING INCOME	17.2%	15.9%	20.4%
Interest Expense	0.8%	0.9%	1.0%
Interest Income	0.1%	0.1%	0.1%
Other nonoperating income, net	1.1%	0.2%	0.3%
EARNINGS FROM CONTINUING OPERATIONS	17.6%	15.3%	19.8%
Income Taxes on Continuing Operations	4.1%	4.1%	4.0%
NET EARNINGS FROM CONTINUING OPERATIONS	13.5%	11.1%	15.8%

Thus, we can see how the company's cost of product sold as a percentage of Sales has increased over the 3-year period (from 48.5 to 50.4 percent). This, along with a one-time goodwill impairment and increase in Selling, General & Administration (SG&A)expenses (31.1 to 32 percent), has led to a ~3 percent fall in Operating Margins. Since there is an increase in nonoperating income (from 0.3 percent of Sales to 1.1 percent), overall Net Earnings have fallen by just 2.3 percent of Sales.

Common Profit Measures

The income statement helps us analyze profits at multiple levels.

Profit measure	Definition	Benefits/comments
Gross margin	Revenues less: Cost Of Goods Sold	• When comparing companies, be sure to understand what's in COGS
EBITDA Earnings before interest, tax, depreciation, and amortization	Gross margin less: operating expenses, except depreciation and amortization	• Often used as approximation of cash flow, e.g. in Discounted Cash Flow analysis
EBITA Earnings before interest, tax, and amortization	EBITDA less: depreciation	• Safe bet when doing cross-border comparisons, given treatment of amortization in different countries
EBIT Earnings before interest and tax	EBITA less: amortization or: Gross margin less operating expenses	• This is what most people mean when they say "operating profit"
NOPAT Net operating profit after tax	EBIT less: tax	• After-tax measure of operating profit • Often used in financial ratios
PBT Profit before tax	EBIT less: interest	• Used by some companies as key profit measure
Net income	EBIT less: interest and tax	• "The bottomline" • Profit that goes to shareholders • Used for earnings per share and P/E multiples

Profitability Analysis—Case of a Publisher

Let us consider the value chain for a book. Based on the Recommended Retail Price (RRP), a 30 percent discount is applied to get the Net Price.

Paper, Printing, and Binding (PPB) is the cost only of the physical book: the amount of money (per book) we will have to spend on the paper, the printing, and the binding process. This, along with freight and royalty, forms the major cost components.

In volumes, there is allowance in quantity printed versus sold because of free samples, book returns, etc.

Thus, we get the Net Sales and reduce the Cost of Goods Sold (COGS) from it to get the net profit (Figure 21).

Pyramid of Ratios

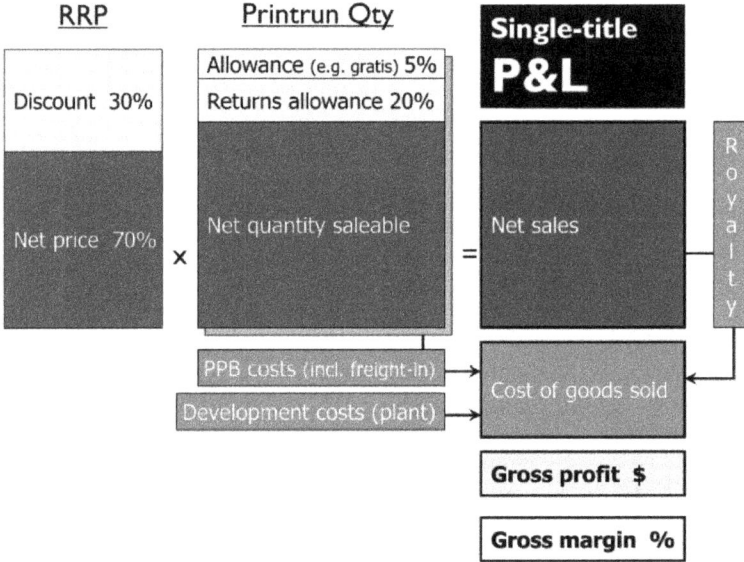

Figure 21

The pyramid of ratios can also be used to analyze the performance of different business units within the same company.

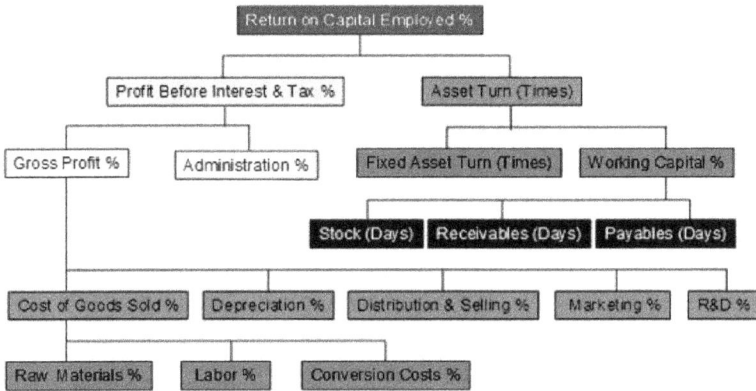

Example for a manufacturing company

Figure 22

Profitability Ratios

It's safe to say that without profitability, a business wouldn't survive in the long run. Profitability ratios help you determine whether a company has the ability to earn a profit in the future. It includes Net Profit Margin, Return on Assets, and Return on Equity and uses elements of both income statements and balance sheets.

Net Profit Margin ratio

The Net Profit Margin ratio—also known as Profit Margin on Sales or Return on Sales (ROS)—measures how well a company can turn sales into net income. It measures management's success in controlling costs and pricing and tells you the net profit per sales dollar after all expenses are deducted from the total sales amount.

To calculate the Net Profit Margin, you divide Net Income by Net Sales.

Although a high profit margin is generally better than a low profit margin, this value shouldn't be analyzed in isolation. It needs to be compared with ratios from previous years with ratios of other companies in the same industry, or with an accepted reference value. Sometimes, a low profit margin is just a part of doing business in a specific industry sector.

Take a company with a net income of $1.45 million and sales of $23.4 million. If you divide $1.45 million by $23.4 million and multiply by 100, the result is a 6.2 percent Net Profit Margin. This means that the company earns a profit of $6.20 for each $100.00 of sales revenue.

Return on Assets (ROA)

However, any company can show a profit. So for more clarity let's use another profitability ratio: the ROA. ROA measures how well a company uses its assets to generate net income. So it indicates which businesses can make good profits with little assets.

It's calculated as Net Income divided by Total Assets.

This formula measures how much profit, after taxes, was earned on the total capital contributed by creditors and owners. So, like Net Profit Margin, the higher the ROA, the better. So if a business has earned $375,000 in net income on $2,500,000 in assets, the ROA would be $375,000 divided by $2,500,000, which is 0.015. As a percentage, the ROA is 15 percent.

Return on Equity (ROE)

The next ratio is ROE, which measures the return shareholders are receiving on their investment in the company. It lets shareholders gauge management's ability to return money for each dollar they've invested. You can use this ratio to compare the profitability of different companies in the same industry.

The formula is Net Income divided by Shareholders' Equity. As with the other profitability ratios, the general rule for ROE is that higher is better. Shareholders' Equity includes both capital stock and retained earnings. So a Net Income of $2,189,833 divided by a Shareholders' Equity of $7,670,217 would result in 0.28549, or 28.55 percent.

Profitability ratios help you to determine whether a business is able to generate profits from assets, equity, and sales to ensure its long-term survival.

Analyzing Efficiency Ratios

When investing in a business, you're definitely hoping it's profitable and a return will be coming your way. But in your analysis of a company's financial status, give efficiency ratios some room at the table as well. They're used for measuring management's effectiveness in managing assets and liabilities to generate revenues and profits.

To calculate efficiency ratios, you use information from income statements, Cash Flow Statements, and Balance Sheets.

You'll get the most benefit from using efficiency ratios when you use them to compare businesses in the same industry.

Receivables Turnover Ratio

The first efficiency ratio is Receivables Turnover ratio, which measures how many times a company's accounts receivable turn over in a period—typically 1 year. When companies extend credit to clients, it results in accounts receivable.

So how's it calculated? You divide Net Credit Sales for the year by the Average Accounts Receivable for the year. Only credit sales should be included in the net sales figure.

Generally, a higher receivables turnover is better, since that means there's a shorter time to collect. A simple evaluation is for management to take the average number of days taken by customers to pay debts and compare it with the number of days in the credit terms. For example, an average collection period of 33.46 days would indicate good efficiency for payment terms of 45 days for credit sales.

Inventory Turnover Ratio

The second ratio is the Inventory Turnover Ratio, which measures the number of times a company sells and replaces its inventory in a given period. It indicates how fast a company can sell its goods. And it is useful because it helps manage "frozen cash," which is cash invested in in-process and finished inventories.

It's calculated with the formula COGS divided by the Average Inventory. The higher the turnover, the better. The goal is for the Inventory Turnover Ratio to increase over time so that there's less investment in stock. The turnover rate should be high enough for cash to come in from customers before suppliers need to be paid.

Operating Cash Flow to Sales Ratio

The third ratio is the Operating Cash Flow to Sales Ratio, which gives you an idea of a company's efficiency in turning sales into cash. It's expressed as a percentage and shows the relationship between cash generated from operations and sales made over a specified period.

Operating cash flow is the net cash generated from operations, which includes both net income and changes in working capital. It's found on the cash flow statement.

The formula used is Operating Cash Flow divided by Net Sales, which is found on the income statement.

Cash is just as important as profit because a company needs cash to pay dividends, suppliers, and creditors, and to purchase assets. The higher the Operating Cash Flow to Sales Ratio, the better. After all, a company's sales and operating cash flow should grow in parallel.

Efficiency ratios let you analyze the efficiency of a company's management of resources and investments.

Liquidity Ratio Analysis

Liquidity brings to mind the idea of flowing water. In finance, liquidity means having cash, as well as the ability to quickly convert assets into cash. For a business, this means cash flows freely enough so it can pay off its current liabilities quickly with what it has. Liquidity ratios, which are sometimes called working capital ratios, measure the availability of cash.

When thinking about liquidity, you should also consider solvency. Solvency is all about business risk. For example, the inability of business to pay off debts and investments from its assets and cash flow in the long term. Both liquidity and solvency ratios use elements of the balance sheet: a statement of financial position, which gives a snapshot of a company at a given point in time. It typically lists assets, liabilities, and capital.

Liquidity ratios measure the short-term solvency of a business, gauging the company's ability to meet its credit obligations. There are two commonly used liquidity ratios.

Current Ratio

The Current ratio expresses how well a company is able to pay its creditors from its current assets. As one of the best-known measures of financial strength, it answers the question "Are there are enough current assets to meet the current liabilities with a margin of safety?" It's worth mentioning that current assets are assumed to be convertible into cash within 1 year, and current liabilities are short-term debts that are due in 1 year or less.

The formula is Current Assets divided by Current Liabilities.

In general, a Current ratio of around 2.0 is good for a lender or creditor. Higher or lower values might be a cause for concern.

Acid Test Ratio

You know that the Current ratio includes all Current Assets. The Acid Test ratio includes only the most liquid current assets. It's also called the Quick ratio because it includes only cash and current assets that can quickly be converted to cash. It's more accurate in measuring true liquidity because it doesn't include inventory and prepaid expenses. This ratio answers the question, "If all sales income were to stop, could the business still meet its current obligations with the quickly convertible funds it has on hand?"

It's calculated with the formula Liquid Assets divided by Current Liabilities. Liquid assets are cash, marketable securities, and accounts receivable. As a rough guide, the Acid Test ratio should be 1.0 or higher. When the ratio is 1.0, it means that liquid assets are pretty much equal to the liabilities owed. So the company can pay what it owes without needing to sell its inventory.

But what does it mean if it is less than 1.0? Possibly, the company isn't solvent for the short term. But, in some industries, 0.7 might be acceptable. These companies have liquid assets available to cover just less than three-quarters of the current liabilities.

So a company that is highly liquid inspires confidence as their short-term financial situation is secure.

Analyzing Solvency Ratios

It takes hard work to pay off debts for both businesses and individuals. In financial terms, solvency means being able to pay all legal debts even if you have to convert assets to cash. Basically, debts can be dissolved by the assets. Liquidity ratios relate to what's currently happening. But solvency ratios take a longer-term approach and help you determine whether a company is financially overextended. There are two commonly used solvency ratios, which both use elements of the balance sheet.

Debt to Total Assets

The first one—Debt to Total Assets—includes both short-term and long-term debt as well as tangible and intangible assets. It's calculated by adding up the company's Total Debt and then dividing by Total Assets. This ratio measures the percentage of assets financed by creditors, as opposed to the percentage financed by owners. It gives you an idea of a company's ability to withstand losses while still being able to cover its obligations.

A high Debt to Total Assets ratio might be a red flag that the business may not be able to meet its long-term obligations. This business might be called highly debt leveraged. A ratio under 1.0 means that most assets are financed through equity and earnings, whereas a ratio above 1.0 means they're financed more by debt.

For example, total liabilities of $110,000 divided by total assets of $200,000 gives you a ratio of 0.55. This isn't bad—about half of the company's assets are financed through equity. But it could also indicate a conservative approach to opportunities for leveraging on potentially low-interest debts.

Debt to Equity Ratio

The Debt to Equity ratio, on the other hand, compares debt to owners' equity instead of comparing debt to assets. When you calculate how much the company is leveraged in debt, you can find the relationship between what is owed and what is owned.

The shareholders'—or owners'—equity is the claim stockholders have to a company's assets once all creditors and debtors have been paid. It's the company's net worth, and it's calculated by subtracting total liabilities from total assets. The Debt to Equity ratio is the tool that highlights the extent to which debt is covered by shareholders' funds.

The formula for the Debt to Equity ratio is Total Liabilities divided by Total Shareholders' Equity. Sometimes, only interest-bearing, long-term debts are considered instead of total liabilities in the calculation.

For example, a Total Liabilities of $110,000 divided by the Total Shareholders' Equity of $90,000 results in a ratio of 1.22. This is a relatively high ratio.

As a rule of thumb, a high Debt to Equity ratio may indicate high risks—such as interest rate increases and creditor nervousness—and even financial weakness. The company may have been too aggressive in financing its growth with debt.

You can now use the power of solvency ratios to check whether a company's longer-term obligations can be met easily or not.

Others

Other commonly used comparative measures of company performance include:

A) Total Shareholder Return (TSR)—dividends in the period plus the change in the share price over the period divided by the share price at the start of the period

B) ROE—earnings in the period divided by the book value of shareholder funds at the period end date

C) Earnings per Share (EPS)—earnings for the period divided by the number of shares in circulation at the period end date

D) Dividend yield (DY)—dividends declared in the period divided by the prevailing share price

Illustration

X Co. has made plans for the next year. It is estimated that the company will employ total assets of $8,00,000, 50 percent of the assets being financed by borrowed capital at an interest cost of 8 percent per year. The direct costs for the year are estimated at $4,80,000, and all other operating expenses are estimated at $80,000. The goods will be sold to customers at 150 percent of the direct costs. Tax rate is assumed to be 50 percent.

You are required to *calculate*: (i) net profit margin, (ii) ROA, (iii) asset turnover, and (iv) return on owners' equity.

The net profit is calculated as follows:

Sales (150% of 4,80,000)		7,20,000
Direct costs		4,80,000
Gross profit		2,40,000
Operating expenses	80,000	
Interest changes (8% of 4,00,000)	32,000	1,12,000
Profit before taxes		1,28,000
Taxes (@ 50%)		64,000
Net profit after taxes		64,000

I. Net profit margin = Profit after taxes/Sales = 64,000/7,20,000 = 0.89 or 8.9%

   Net profit margin = EBIT $(1-T)$/Sales = 1,60,000$(1-0.5)$/7,20,000 = 0.111 or 11.1%

II. ROA = EBIT $(1-T)$/Assets = 1,60,000$(1-0.5)$/8,00,000 = 0.10 or 10%

III. Asset turnover = Sales/Assets = 7,20,000/8,00,000 = 0.9

IV. ROE = Net Profit after taxes/Owners' equity = 64,000/50% of 8,00,000 = 64,000/4,00,000 = 0.16 or 16%

Du Pont Analysis

The Du Pont analysis computes the ROE as the product of margin, turnover, and leverage:

ROE = Net profit margin $\times$ Total asset turnover $\times$ Equity multiplier

Profit margin shows the operating efficiency, asset turnover shows the asset use efficiency, and leverage factor shows how much leverage is being used.

We can rewrite the Du Pont relationship using the ratio formulas as follows:

$$ROE = \frac{Net\ income}{Sales} \times \frac{Sales}{Total\ assets} \times \frac{1}{1 - \dfrac{Total\ debt}{Total\ assets}}$$

There is nothing very complicated about this equation.

If we break it up further, we get Net Income divided by Equity, which is just the equation for the ROE. However, it is extremely useful as a tool to establish a beginning point for analysis. Whether the ROE is declining, or not as high as the firm's competitors, determines whether the problems are with the margin, turnover, or leverage of the firm.

Note that high leverage may mask problems with margin and turnover. Once you have located the problem, examine the inputs to the troublesome ratio for additional clues. For example, if total asset turnover is declining, is it because sales have dropped or because the firm has acquired additional assets?

Figure 23 can be used to track the source of the problem through ratios.

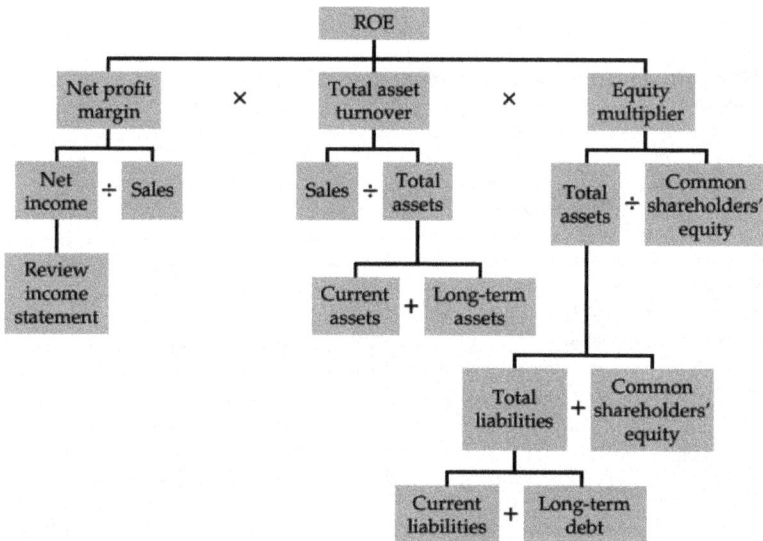

Figure 23

Illustration—Amazon's DuPont Analysis

Download its financial statements from http://financials.morningstar.com/ into Excel. In the box on this web page, enter the company name and click on Go. You will get the company's income statement. Toward the top right, you will see Export. Click on the icon right below it to import the income statement into Excel. Toward the top left of the page (right below the company's name), you will see Balance Sheet and Cash Flow. Click on one, export it to Excel, as you did for the income statement, and do the same for the last financial statement. Once you have done this, calculate the ROE in each of the 5 years for Amazon.

Now, maybe you can pick up a competitor and check why Amazon is doing better or worse than this competitor?

Two-Component Disaggregation of ROE

	ROE	=	ROA	×	Financial Leverage
Dec 31, 2019	18.67%		5.14%		3.63
Dec 31, 2018	23.13%		6.19%		3.73
Dec 31, 2017	10.95%		2.31%		4.74
Dec 31, 2016	12.29%		2.84%		4.32
Dec 31, 2015	4.45%		0.91%		4.89

Amazon.com Inc. - Three-Component Disaggregation of ROE

	ROE	= Net Profit Margin	× Asset Turnover	× Financial Leverage
Dec 31, 2019	18.67%	4.13%	1.25	3.63
Dec 31, 2018	23.13%	4.33%	1.43	3.73
Dec 31, 2017	10.95%	1.71%	1.35	4.74
Dec 31, 2016	12.29%	1.74%	1.63	4.32
Dec 31, 2015	4.45%	0.56%	1.64	4.89

Based on: 10-K (filing date: 2020-01-31), 10-K (filing date: 2019-02-01), 10-K (filing date: 2018-02-02), 10-K (filing date: 2017-02-10), 10-K (filing date: 2016-01-29).

This can be further broken into five-component analysis.

	ROE	= Tax Burden	× Interest Burden	× EBIT Margin	× Asset Turnover	× Financial Leverage
Dec 31, 2019	18.67%	0.83	0.90	5.55%	1.25	3.63
Dec 31, 2018	23.13%	0.89	0.89	5.45%	1.43	3.73
Dec 31, 2017	10.95%	0.80	0.82	2.61%	1.35	4.74
Dec 31, 2016	12.29%	0.62	0.89	3.15%	1.63	4.32
Dec 31, 2015	4.45%	0.39	0.77	1.87%	1.64	4.89

The primary reason for the decrease in ROE over the year 2019 is the decrease in efficiency measured by the asset turnover ratio.

CHAPTER 3

Management Accounting

Financial Accounting versus Management Accounting

Financial accounts are historic, and most of the information that is provided is financial in nature.

In contrast, management accounts are used to help management record, plan, and control the activities of a business and to assist in the decision-making and decision-taking processes. They can be prepared for any period of time such as daily, weekly, monthly, or yearly. Reports can be both forward looking or historic or a mix of both.

While there is no legal requirement to prepare management accounts, few businesses could expect to survive or thrive without them. Management accounts are prepared to meet the specific needs of the user and typically include both financial and non-financial information. There are an infinite number of potential management reports a business could choose, for example

- Profit and loss showing actual versus forecast budget performance including this year versus last year to date and year to go
- Sales and margin report by business unit, product, or service or by customer type and/or by specific customer
- Number of employees, employee costs, and productivity
- Customer service levels by customer, by depot, and by product type

Fixed Costs

Fixed costs remain fairly constant, regardless of production or sales volumes during the budget period. Examples include

- Rent
- Basic utilities, including electric and telephone service
- Equipment leases

- Depreciation
- Interest payments
- Administrative costs
- Marketing and advertising
- Indirect labor, such as salaried supervisory employees

Variable Costs

Variable costs change in direct proportion to shifts in production or sales volumes during the budget period. Examples include

- Raw materials
- Direct labor
- Packaging
- Energy (electricity, gas) used in manufacturing or production
- Shipping
- Sales commissions
- Income taxes

Your estimates of the variable costs that will be incurred during the budget period depend on your group's or organization's plans. By understanding those plans, you can anticipate the need for resources (such as expanded capacity) and include them in your budget requests (Figures 24 and 25).

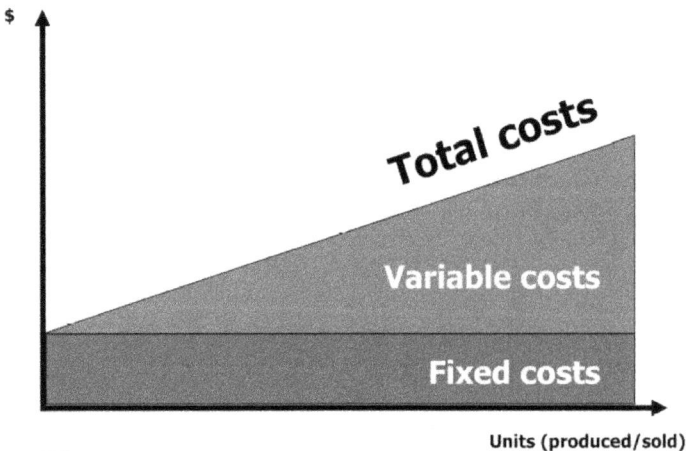

Figure 24

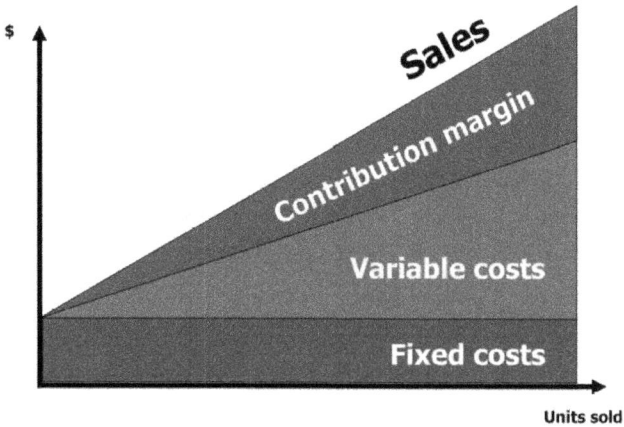

Figure 25

If Variable Cost is deducted from the Sales Price, the amount left is Contribution to Fixed Costs. Contribution is the difference between Price and the Variable Costs of a product or service. A product is worth making and selling if it makes a contribution to Fixed Costs (Figure 26).

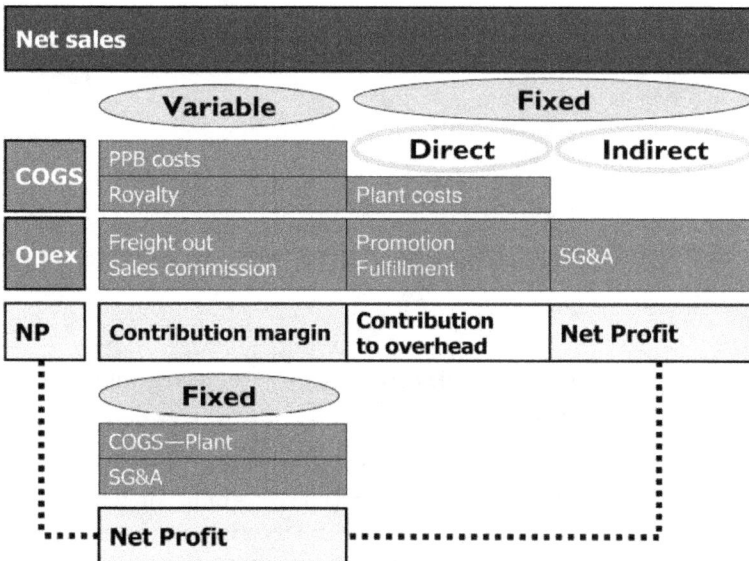

Figure 26

Based on the Recommended Retail Price (RRP), a 30 percent discount is applied to get the Net Sales Price.

PPB is the cost only of the physical book: how much money (per book) we will have to spend on the paper, the printing, and the binding process. This, along with freight, commission, and royalty, forms the major variable cost components. COGS comprises PPB and Royalty. Freight and commission are Operating Costs.

What we get is Contribution, from which we reduce the Direct & Indirect Fixed Costs of the publishing setup to arrive at the Net profit.

Application of Management Accounting in Decision Making

Now let us consider certain decision-making situations

Make-or Buy-Decisions

The make-or-buy decision is the act of making a strategic choice between producing an item internally (in-house) and buying it externally (from an outside vendor)

A key consideration here is spare capacity

Key principles are as follows:

If spare production capacity is available, we have spare room to *make* more products, and therefore

- Production resources may be idle (if the component is purchased from outside)
- Fixed costs are irrelevant (because we won't need any extra fixed costs)

So just consider the variable costs of *making* compared with the purchase cost of *buying*

We must *buy* if the buying price < the variable costs of making

We must *make* if buying price > variable costs of making

No spare capacity available?

So we need to buy more space or stop making something to create space

Stopping making something to create capacity causes lost contribution

So compare the contribution lost + extra costs of *making* with the purchase price of *buying*

Decision

Buy if relevant costs of making > Purchase price

Make if relevant costs of making < Purchase price

Relevant Costs

Make-or-buy decisions must be based on the relevant cost of each option.

Relevant costs in make-or-buy decisions include all incremental cash flows.

Any cost that does not change as a result of the decision should be ignored, such as depreciation and indirect fixed costs.

Calculating the relevant cost is the first step in finding the most cost-effective option.

The following are examples of relevant costs in make-or-buy decisions:

Relevant Costs	Examples
Variable costs	Cost of labor involved in the production.
	Cost of material used in manufacturing.
	Variable production overheads such as the cost of electricity used in production.
Direct fixed costs	Rent of production facility.
	Salary of factory supervisor.
Opportunity cost	Rental income from machinery that is given up for manufacturing in-house.

Examples of irrelevant costs in make-or-buy decisions are as follows:

Non-Relevant Costs	Examples
Indirect fixed costs	General and administrative expense.
Non-cash expenses	Depreciation.
Sunk costs	Cost of machinery already paid.
Committed costs	The rental expense of a factory building

Once we sort out the relevant costs in the make-or-buy decision, we need to find which option minimizes the total cost.

Illustration

Craft Ltd makes four components, A, B, C, and D, and the associated annual costs are as follows:

	A	B	C	D
Production volume (units)	1,500	3,000	5,000	7,000
Unit variable costs	$	$	$	$
Direct Materials	4	4	5	5
Direct Labor	8	8	6	6
Variable production overheads	2	1	4	5
Total	14	13	15	16
Fixed costs directly attributable are:	3,000	6,000	10,000	7,000
The unit prices of an external supplier are:	12	16	20	24

Determine whether any of the components should be bought in from the external supplier.

Solution

	A	B	C	D
Costs if Made	14	13	15	16
Costs if Bought	−12	−16	−20	−24
Savings per unit Bought	2	−3	−5	−8
Number of units	1,500	3,000	5,000	7,000
Total Savings if Bought	3,000	−9,000	−25,000	−56,000
Plus Direct Fixed Costs Saved	3,000	6,000	10,000	7,000
Total Saving	6,000	−3,000	−15,000	−49,000

Therefore only buy in component A, because this is the only one that makes a saving if bought in.

Illustration

DBA manufactures and sells 25,000 table fans annually. One of the components required for fans is purchased from an outside supplier at a price of $190 per unit. Annually, it purchases 25,000 components for its usage. The production manager is of the opinion that if all the components are produced at their own plant, it is possible to maintain better quality of the finished product. Further, he proposes that the in-house production of the component with other items will provide more flexibility to increase the annual production by another 5,000 units. He estimates the cost of making the component as follows:

Direct materials	$80
Direct labor	$75
Factory overhead (70% variable)	$40
Total cost	$195

The proposal of the production manager is referred to the marketing manager for his remarks. He points out that to market the additional units, the overall unit price should be reduced by 5 percent and, additionally, $1,00,000 per month should be incurred on advertising. The present selling price and contribution per fan are $2,500 and $600, respectively. No other increase or decrease in all other expenses as a result of this proposal will arise.

Since the making cost of the component is more than the buying cost, the management asks you to:

I. *analyze* the make-or-buy decision on unit basis and total basis.
II. *recommend* the most profitable alternative.

Solution

DBA purchases 25,000 units of components to manufacture 25,000 fans annually. The external purchase price per component is $190 per unit. It has the option of manufacturing these components in-house. The cost structure of manufacturing these components would be as follows:

Cost structure	Cost per component unit ($)
Direct Materials	80
Direct Labor	75
Variable Factory Overhead (70% of $40)	28
Total	183

Analysis

If DBA decides to manufacture the components in-house, the following would be the financial impact:

A) Production capacity will increase from 25,000 fans to 30,000 fans.

B) Variable cost of production of fans would be $1,710 ($2,500–$600)–$190) per unit.

C) Fixed factory overhead of $12 per component would be incurred irrespective of whether the component is produced or not. Therefore, this cost is not considered.

D) Increase in advertising expense would be $100,000 per month, or $12,00,000 annually.

E) Overall selling price would reduce from the current rate of $2,500 per fan to $2,375 (95 percent of $2,500) per fan.

F) Current contribution considering a procurement price of $190 per component unit is $600 per fan. As calculated previously, if produced in-house, the variable cost would be $183 per component unit. This would result in an increase in contribution by $7 per fan (procurement price of $190 per component unit less variable cost of $183 per component unit). In addition, there is an impact of $125 on account of reduction in selling price. Therefore, the contribution if the components are produced in-house would be $482 per fan ($600 + $7–$125).

To summarize the above figures:

	Procurement 25,000 components		Produce 30,000 components	
	Per fan $	Total $	Per fan $	Total $
Selling price per fan	2,500	6,25,00,000	2,375	7,12,50,000
Contribution per fan	600	1,50,00,000	482	1,44,60,000

Therefore, incremental loss by switching to in-house production (on a total basis) would be **$17,40,000** (incremental loss $5,40,000 – additional advertising expenses $12,00,000). On a per unit basis, it would result in a **loss of $58 per fan**.

Recommendation

As explained earlier, if production increases from 25,000 fans to 30,000 fans, it would not be profitable to make these components in-house. Overall profit decreased by $17,40,000. However, DBA may prefer to make the components, even though it could be financially beneficial to buy them from an outside supplier. Sometimes, qualitative factors become very important and can override some financial benefit. This can be coupled with uncertainty about the supplier's ability or intention to maintain the price, quality, and delivery dates of the components, etc.

Alternatively, DBA may continue with the sale of 25,000 units without any price reduction and advertising expenses. The components required for the 25,000 fans may be produced internally at a cost of $183 per unit. In this situation, the contribution shall be increased by $ 175,000 ($7 × 25,000 units).

Thus, DBA may choose the alternative after due and careful consideration of the facts illustrated previously.

Whether or Not to Process Further

Should a business sell its product immediately, or should it sell them at a premium after further processing?

In situations where a decision has to be made as to whether joint products are sold at the split-off point or, alternatively, processed further before being sold, relevant cost principles apply.

Key principles are as follows:

A) the apportionment of common costs is irrelevant in decisions concerning whether or not to process individual products further. Common costs are relevant only to decisions about the process as a whole.

B) decisions about whether or not to process further should be made on the basis of incremental revenue (final sales value after further processing less the sales value at the split-off point) less incremental cost (the cost of processing further).

Joint products A and B result from a single manufacturing process. Each product could be sold at the split-off point or, alternatively, processed further.

Illustration

A farmer is planning for the upcoming harvest of grapes.
The estimated production of fresh grapes for this season is 10 MT.
He will spend $2,000 on preharvest expenses for preparing the crop.
Two options are available to the farmer for selling grapes.

Option A

Sell fresh grapes to retailers.
The expected selling price of fresh grapes is $1,500/MT.
Packaging would cost $200/MT.
Transportation cost is estimated at $300/MT.

Option B

The farmer can dehydrate the fresh grapes in summer and sell them as
  dry grapes in winter.
10 MT of fresh grapes can be processed into 2 MT of dry grapes.
The price of dry grapes in winter is estimated at $12,000/MT.
The cost of the dehydration process is $500/MT of fresh grapes.
Packaging and storage of dry grapes cost $3,000/MT.
Transportation cost of dry grapes is $500/MT.

Calculate Which Option Will Maximize Lisa's Profit

We need to compare the incremental revenue of each option with its incremental cost.

	Option A Immediate Sale	Option B Further Process
Sales Revenue	15,000 [$1,500 × 10 MT]	24,000 [$12,000 × 2 MT]
Processing Cost	-	(5,000) [$500 × 10 MT]
Packaging & storage	2,000 ($200 × 10 MT)	(6,000) [$3,000 × 2 MT]
Transport	3,000 ($300 × 10 MT)	(1,000) [$500 × 2 MT]
Total cost	10,000	12,000

Option B is more profitable.

Preharvest costs are unavoidable and therefore ignored in the calculation.

Illustration

The following data about the two products are available:

	$ per unit	
	Product A	Product B
Share of common costs from joint process	25.20	25.20
Selling price at split-off point	24.00	38.40
Cost of further processing	8.60	12.20
Selling price after further processing	32.00	48.40

Which product(s) should be sold at the split-off point?

A) Both products
B) Product A only
C) Product B only
D) Neither product

Solution

A product should be sold at the split-off point if there is no incremental profit from processing the product further. As long as the process as a whole is profitable, it is irrelevant if an individual product is not profitable. It has to be assumed, in this example, that the process as a whole is profitable.

The incremental profit/loss from further processing is calculated as follows:

	$ per unit	
	Product A	**Product B**
Incremental revenue	8.00 (32.00 – 24.00)	10.00 (48.40 – 38.40)
Incremental cost	8.60	12.20
Incremental profit/loss	(0.60)	(2.20)
Selling price after further processing	32.00	48.40

Both products, therefore, should be sold at the split-off point (option A) because further processing of either product is not financially justified. In the December 2011 Paper MA2 exam, only 23 percent of candidates reached this conclusion.

Shutdown Problems

Here you need to look at the following:

The loss in revenue from closing down the operation, and

The saving in costs from closing down (= avoidable costs).

This basically means look at its contribution—so make sure all the costs are direct—otherwise they won't be saved.

This sort of question is asking for a decision as to whether or not to close part of the business.

Illustration

A) A company manufactures three products, Pawns, Rooks, and Bishops. The present net annual income from these is as follows:

(in $)	Pawns	Rooks	Bishops	Total
Sales	50,000	40,000	60,000	150,000
Less variable costs	30,000	25,000	35,000	90,000
Contribution	20,000	15,000	25,000	60,000
Less fixed costs	17,000	18,000	20,000	55,000
Profit/loss	3,000	(3,000)	5,000	5,000

The company is considering whether or not to cease selling Rooks. It is felt that selling prices cannot be raised or lowered without adversely affecting net income. $5,000 of the fixed costs of Rooks are direct fixed costs that would be saved if production ceased. All other fixed costs would remain the same.

B) Suppose, however, that it were possible to use the resources released by stopping production of Rooks to produce a new item, Crowners, which would sell for $50,000 and incur variable costs of $30,000 and extra direct fixed costs of $6,000.

Consider whether the company should cease production and sale of Rooks under each of the scenarios in (A) and (B).

Illustration

The management of ABC It's all going wrong! Co is considering the closure of one of its operations (department 2), and the financial accountant has submitted the following report.

Department	1	2	3	Total
Sales (units)	10,000	5,000	15,000	30,000
Sales ($)	1,50,000	92,000	1,58,000	4,00,000
Direct material	75,000	75,000	50,000	2,00,000
Direct labor	25,000	25,000	10,000	60,000
Production overhead	5,000	2,500	7,500	15,000
Gross profit	45,000	−10,500	90,500	1,25,000
Expenses	−15,000	−9,200	−15,800	−40,000
Net profit ($)	30,000	−19,700	74,700	85,000

In addition to the information supplied previously, you are told that
Production overheads of $15,000 have been apportioned to the three departments on the basis of unit sales volume.

Expenses are head office overhead, apportioned to departments on sales value.

As management accountant, you further ascertain that on a cost driver basis

Half of the so-called direct labor is fixed and cannot be readily allocated.

Prepare a report for management including a restatement of the financial position in terms of contribution made by each department and making a clear recommendation.

Solution

	1	2	3	Total
Sales	1,50,000	92,000	1,58,000	4,00,000
Direct materials	−75,000	−75,000	−50,000	−2,00,000
Direct labor	−12,500	−12,500	−5,000	−30,000
Production overheads	−5,000	−2,500	−7,500	−15,000
Contribution	57,500	2,000	95,500	1,55,000

As Department 2 makes a positive contribution, it should not be closed down

Shutdown decisions

- Loss of contribution from the segment
- Savings in specific fixed costs from closure
- Penalties resulting from the closure, e.g., redundancy, compensation to customers
- Alternative use for resources released
- Knock-on impact, e.g., loss leaders cancelled—products that got customers into the store

CHAPTER 4

Budgeting

Budgeting

A budget is a document that translates a group's or organizations strategic and operational plans into the expected resources required and returns anticipated over a certain period.

A budget is "[a] quantitative expression of a plan for a defined period of time. It may include planned sales volumes and revenues, resource quantities, costs and expenses, assets, liabilities and cash flows" (CIMA Official Terminology, 2005).

Why Budgets Matter

A budget functions as financial blueprint or action plan that a group or organization creates to ensure it has enough resources to achieve its goals. The budget also helps ensure that achieving those goals generates the desired benefits.

Corporate decisions are all about the choice among the alternative paths faced by the management. We can broadly divide those choices into endogenous alternatives or exogenous alternatives.

A) Endogenous alternatives for value maximization take into consideration the natural growth of the existing family or products.
   - Maybe revising the marketing approach and investing more in the communication with the company's clients via social media, or
   - Maybe revising production procedures in order to reduce forecasted capital or labor costs.

B) The second approach takes into consideration exogenous decisions.
- Should a company develop new products for the existing market, or should it try a new market with its existing, well-established products.
- Should a company go international or should it remain local?
- Should a company buy a competitor or should it spin off an existing division and sell it to the competitor, leaving the market?

All those decisions are corporate decisions, and, as said, they are permanently driven by the pursuit of shareholders' value maximization.

The planning cycle begins with, first, the correct assessment of the corporate, current value and, second, with a clear definition of the potential alternatives for value maximization. Having decided, we eliminate the worst alternatives from a decision making perspective?

The board, the CEO, will request a deeper study of each one of them. That is budgeting, and that is why it is so important to have a well-structured technique for budgeting—because a broad guess can lead the company to disaster. If you do not trust me, if we analyze the decisions made in the 1980s, there were so many errors that they that led the companies to bankruptcy. They were based on a poor understanding of the real forecast, demand, revenues, cost, and capital. At the end of the day, it will be the budgeting technique that will drive resource allocation. The alternative plan that proves to have the higher value for shareholders will be chosen. Capital allocation will be made in favor of those alternatives with the better balance between risk and return.

The decision cycle should be made every year, but usually only once a year.

Managers must have time to implement their decision and observe results. If they spend all their time planning and revising the previous plan, they will not have time to execute the decisions made.

Naturally, along with the implementation phase, monitoring and control come into place. The comparison between expected results and those actually observed will lead to permanent revisions of the decisions made. This is the planning cycle.

When we get a feedback on the decisions we made earlier, we can use the same as a baseline for the future.

Types of Budgets

There are many types of budgets (Figure 27).

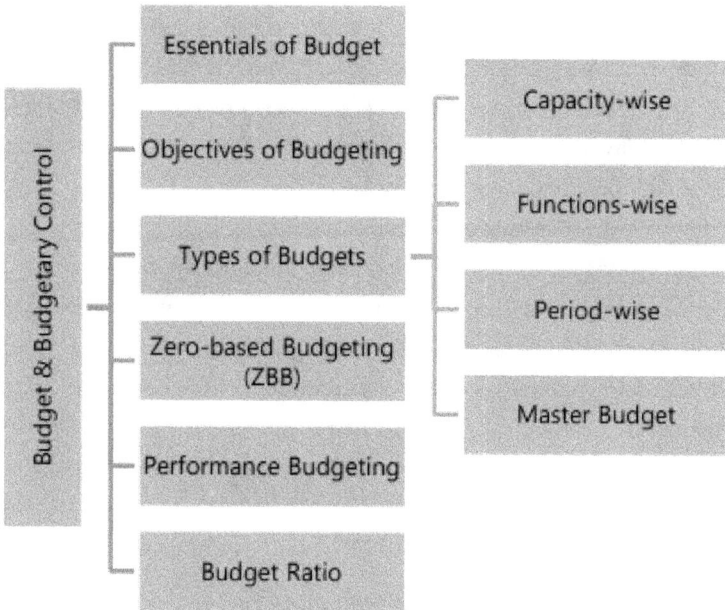

Figure 27

For example:

- **Operating budgets** reflect a group's or organization's day-to-day revenues and expenses. They typically cover a 1-year period.
- **Capital budgets** show planned outlays for investments in plants, equipment, and product development. Capital budgets may cover periods of 3 to 10 years.
- **Cash budgets** plot the expected cash balances an organization will have during the given period, based on information provided in the operating and capital budgets.

As a manager, you may need to prepare operating budgets for your group every year. Your organization's finance department "rolls up" your operating budget and those created by your peers into a master budget for the entire organization.

You may also create capital budgets for investments you're considering making for your group. As with your operating budgets, the finance department combines your capital budgets with other managers' capital budgets to further build the master budget. The operating and capital budget information goes into the balance sheet, and the company's cash flow statement.

You probably won't be preparing cash budgets unless you work in your organization's finance department. That's because this kind of budget is typically created by finance professionals. For that reason, this topic focuses on operating and capital budgets.

Here's a diagram showing the information sources for various organizational budgets—and how the different budgets are connected. In a typical manufacturing company, for instance, the vice presidents of sales, procurement, and manufacturing, along with CFOs, country unit heads, and sales and marketing heads, contribute estimates for the operating budget. The CEO, CFO, division and business unit heads, and plant managers and product managers provide estimates of planned capital investments for the capital budget.

The Seven Steps of Creating an Operating Budget

The Seven Steps of Creating an Operating Budget

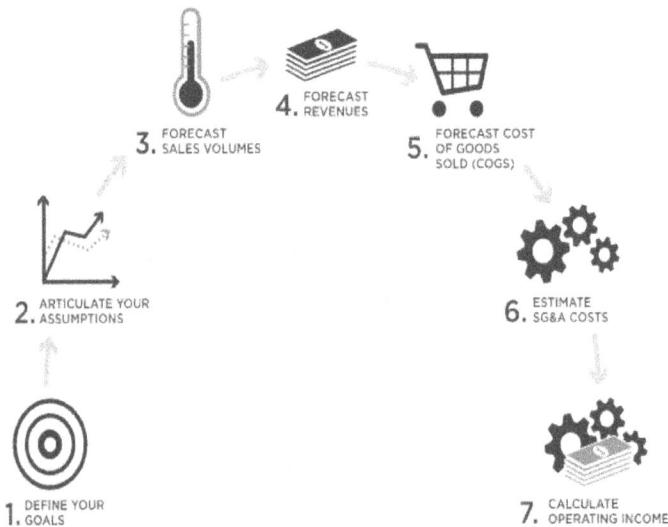

Figure 28

Figure 29

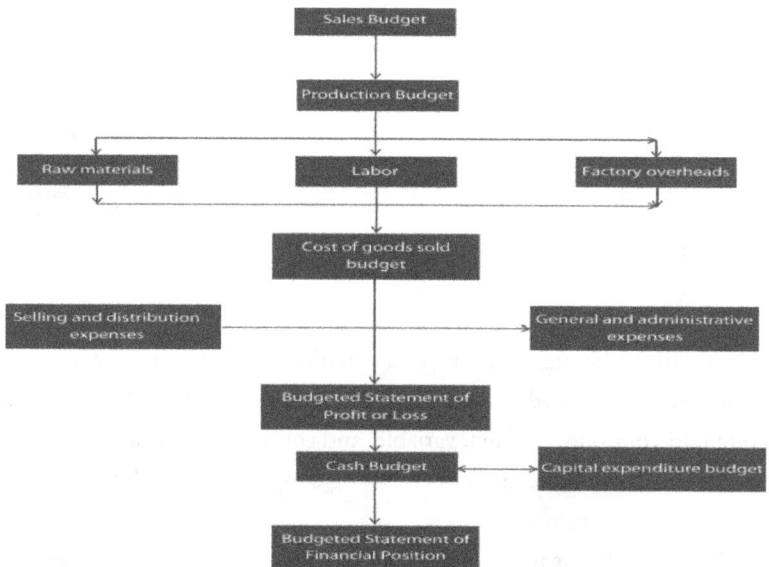

Figure 30

Example

Karl's company's investor relations team might tell analysts

A) "We expect earnings per share of $1.30 to $1.35"
B) "Our capital expenditures won't exceed 10% of our revenues," or
C) "We plan to invest 5% more in R&D over the next 3 years."

Fixed versus Flexible Budgets

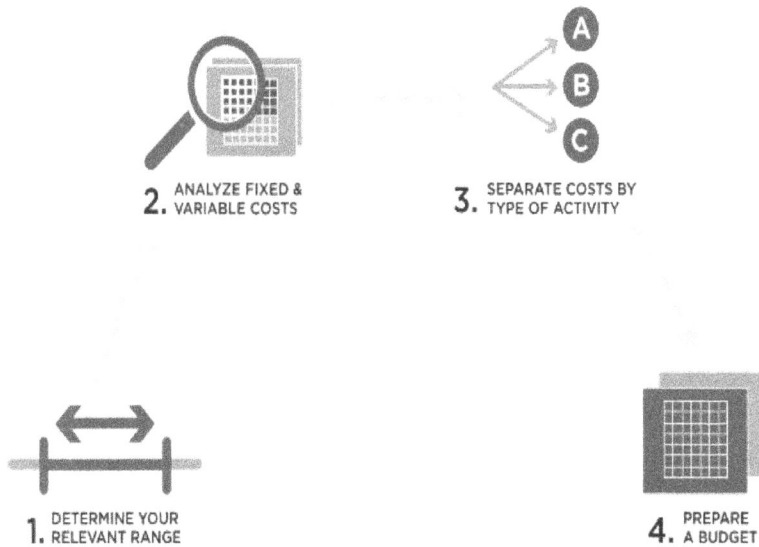

2. ANALYZE FIXED & VARIABLE COSTS

3. SEPARATE COSTS BY TYPE OF ACTIVITY

1. DETERMINE YOUR RELEVANT RANGE

4. PREPARE A BUDGET

Figure 31

Whether your organization takes a traditional or alternative approach to budgeting, you need to distinguish between several types of costs when you build your budget: fixed, variable, and corporate overhead.

There are two basic kinds of operating budgets, fixed and flexible.

A) A fixed budget is used where there are few or no variable expense elements. The manager must stick to the original amount budgeted for the particular budget period (barring a major unforeseen event, such as a labor strike or a weather catastrophe).

B) A **flexible** budget allows the organization to adjust budgeted revenues and costs on the basis of actual levels of activity, which can vary— sometimes greatly. For example, a manager with a flexible budget would be authorized to incur additional production costs to meet unanticipated demand. Flexible budgets are useful where managers have no control over the volume of output; they can spend what they need to meet customers' needs without being penalized for the higher costs.

To build a flexible budget,

1. Determine the relevant range of the activity that is expected to fluctuate during the coming period: the number of widgets manufactured, deliveries run, hours of contractor labor needed, and so forth.
2. Analyze the fixed and variable costs that will be incurred over that range.
3. Separate costs by type of activity, such as market research (for expanding to a new market) or distribution.
4. Prepare a budget showing what costs would be incurred at various points throughout the range.

Example

Demi, a marketing manager for a furniture retailer, is planning a marketing campaign for the next year's new fall line. She will include in her budget the cost of an advertising agency's services, the fees for freelance writers, and the labor costs for additional call center representatives to handle expected increases in call volume.

Flexible budgets are especially valuable for organizations operating in volatile business environments.

Example

Tom is a supply chain manager for a steel manufacturer. Among other things, he is responsible for maintaining inventory at levels that support the sales plan. His company faces numerous uncertainties that could cause actual revenues and costs to differ markedly from those originally budgeted, including:

A) Fluctuations in the supply and cost of raw materials, electricity, and natural gas
B) Sudden changes in market demand for steel products, owing to a volatile global economy
C) Intensifying competitive pressures from imports
D) Changes in foreign trade policy affecting imports and exports
E) New government regulations increasing environmental compliance costs

For this reason, when preparing his annual budget, he includes ranges for the quantity of raw materials needed for production, as well as for shipping and logistics costs for inbound materials and customer orders.

Illustration

A factory that expects to operate 7,000 hours, i.e., at 70 percent level of activity, furnishes details of expenses as under:
Variable expenses 1,260
Semivariable expenses 1,200
Fixed expenses 1,800
The semivariable expenses go up by 10 percent between 85 percent and 95 percent activity and by 20percent above 95 percent activity.
Prepare a flexible budget for 80, 90, and 100 percent activities.

Solution

Head of Account	Control basis	70%	80%	90%	100%
Budgeted hours		7,000	8,000	9,000	10,000
		(₹)	(₹)	(₹)	(₹)
Variable expenses	V	1,260	1,440	1,620	1,800
Semivariable expenses	SV	1,200	1,200	1,320	1,440
Fixed expenses	F	1,800	1,800	1,800	1,800
Total expenses		4,260	4,440	4,740	5,040
Recovery rate per hour		0.61	0.55	0.53	0.50

Conclusion

We notice that the recovery rate at 70 percent activity is INR 0.61 per hour. If in a particular month the factory works 8,000 hours, it will be incorrect to estimate the allowance as INR 4,880 @ INR 0.61. The correct allowance will be INR 4,440, as shown in the table. If the actual expenses are INR 4,500 for this level of activity, the company has not saved any money but has overspent by INR60 (INR 4,500−INR 4,440).

Budgets and Control

Until the early 1970s, world demand grew above the world capacity of supply, so companies would direct efforts into production—how to produce more, how to produce better, how to produce with lower costs. With a world economic crises in the late 1970s and early 1980s, world demands sharply decreased, and we observed an excessive production capacity in relationship to the existing demand. It was the first moment in recent history that companies really had to compete for the same client in the same market.

A budget is a mechanism for partitioning decision rights and for control. It helps in decision management as well as decision control.

Budgeting procedures and techniques provide a realistic substance for decision making.

Let's remember a fundamental concept: What's the goal of the firm? Although many researchers have proposed that alternative points of view, the quote remains.

The goal of the firm is to maximize shareholder's value, but the question is, how? What decision must managers take in order to chase that goal?

To be able to do so, the management must understand

A) First, how much is the company worth today. There are several techniques to determine the company's value, termed valuation techniques. Typically, the company's value is based on the market's value, mainly if the company stocks are traded, or on its potential to provide future free cash flow to its shareholders, which is called fundamental analysis.

B) The second question is, how much can the company be worth in the future? What is the potential future value of the company?

C) So, naturally, the third question will be, what are the alternative possibilities for the company?

Conduct a Sensitivity Analysis

Through sensitivity analysis, you apply "what-if" situations to your budget to see the effect of a potential change on the original data.

Sensitivity analysis lets you test the assumptions in your budgets and explore the potential impact of alternative scenarios or courses of action. It thus makes your budgets even more valuable as tools for planning and making course corrections.

Sensitivity Analysis and Operating Budgets

When you use sensitivity analysis while creating operating budgets, you ask what would happen if important inputs for your budget calculations—such as sales of a product you're responsible for, or the cost of materials that go into the product—turn out to be higher or lower than you expected.

Sensitivity Analysis and Capital Budgets

When used in capital budgeting, sensitivity analysis can help you evaluate the potential of investment opportunities. Net present value (NPV) calculations can play a major role here by helping you gauge the impact of changes in factors such as discount (interest) rates or inflation rates on the relative costs and benefits of investments you're considering.

Variance Analysis: An Illustration

Analyze Variance

All budgets are based on assumptions about what might happen in the future. So actual business results for the future time period stipulated in a particular budget may differ from what was in the budget.

Variance is the difference between the actual results produced by your group and the results you've budgeted for.

A) Cost variance represents the difference between actual costs and expected costs.
B) Revenue variance is the difference between actual revenues and expected revenues.

Variance can be favorable; for example, sales increase more than anticipated, or a capital investment delivers a greater return than originally calculated. Variance can also be unfavorable; for instance, costs exceed projections, or a capital investment delivers an unexpectedly low return.

Keep in mind that unfavorable variances are not always bad for business: An unexpected increase in spending might well mean an increase in demand for your products or services (Figure 32).

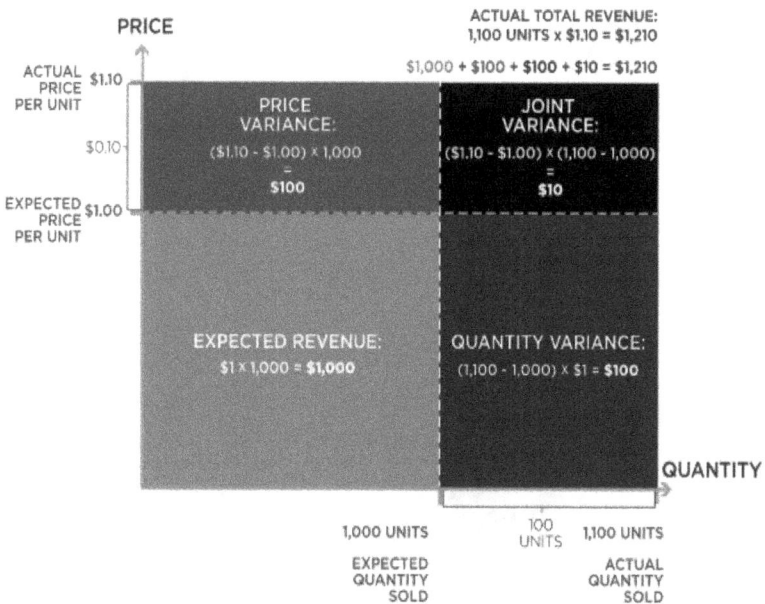

Figure 32

CHAPTER 5

Working Capital Management

Concept

Working capital is the cash needed to finance the day-to-day operations of the business and to

- Pay suppliers for goods and services
- Pay employees
- Pay for inventory and work in progress (WIP)
- Allow customers to buy now, but pay later
- Pay other creditors i.e., taxes to Her Majesty's Revenue and Customs (HMRC) and dividends to shareholders

The working capital cycle or cash cycle is measured in days. It is calculated in three parts:

- Receivables (or debtors) days—this is the average number of days credit is given to customers and is calculated by dividing the period-end value for trade debtors (i.e., the cash due to be received from customers at the period end date) from the balance sheet by the revenue for the year and multiplying by 365.
- Inventory and WIP days—this is the average amount of cash tied up in inventory and work in progress during the year and is calculated by dividing the period end value for inventory and work in progress from the balance sheet by the cost of sales for the year and multiplying by 365.
- Payables (or creditors) days—this is the average number of days credit is given by suppliers and is calculated by dividing the period end value for trade creditors (i.e., the cash due to be paid to

suppliers at the period end) from the balance sheet by the cost of sales for the year and multiplying by 365 (Figure 33).

WORKING CAPITAL CYCLE

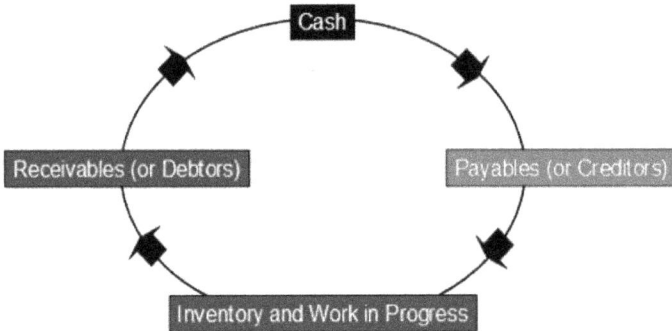

Figure 33

The cash cycle is calculated by adding the number of receivables (debtors) days to the number of inventory and WIP days and then subtracting the number of payables (creditors) days. The larger the number of days in the cash cycle, the more cash that is 'tied up' financing a company's day-to-day operations. Companies generally aim to shorten their cash cycle to free up cash for other uses, i.e., to finance additional investment or to reduce borrowings.

Case Study: Cash Conversion Cycle of a Publisher

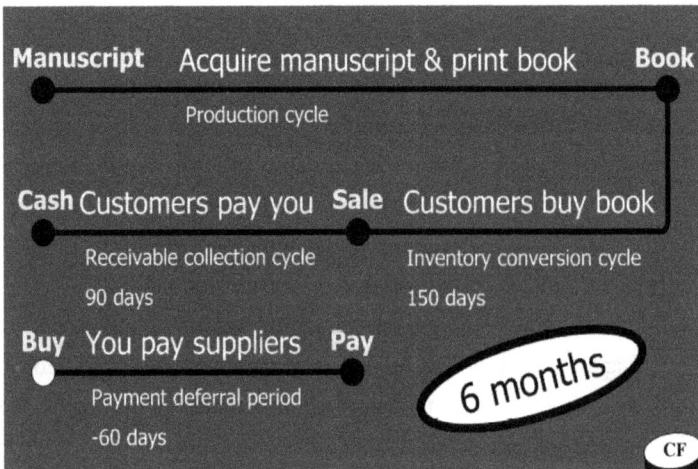

Figure 34

The cash cycle can be reduced by:

- Reducing the number of days credit is given to customers (i.e., invoices are paid more promptly)
- Reducing the amount of inventory and WIP
- Increasing the number of days credit is given by suppliers (i.e., invoices payments are delayed)

More important than making a profit is the ability of a company to convert profit into cash. This requires a business to actively manage its working capital. This is especially the case when undergoing periods of rapid expansion or contraction, both of which can put a severe strain on a company's management and cash flow.

CHAPTER 6

Pricing

Importance of Pricing

Pricing is a business-critical decision and one where for many companies there is considerable scope for improving economic performance.

Once a company has set its pricing objectives, it has to figure out how to achieve them. These decisions form part of the company's pricing strategy.

Although often overlooked, pricing is the most important part of value engineering. This is because price is the only element of the marketing mix that directly produces revenue; all the other elements produce cost.

Price too high	Price too low
Drive customer away	Limited profit margin
	Negative effect on how customer perceives the product quality

Small changes in price can have significant effects on volume, market share, and profitability. In fact, pricing has the highest impact on increasing profit.

Thus, we can see that a 1 percent increase in price leads to an 8 percent increase in profit (Figure 35).

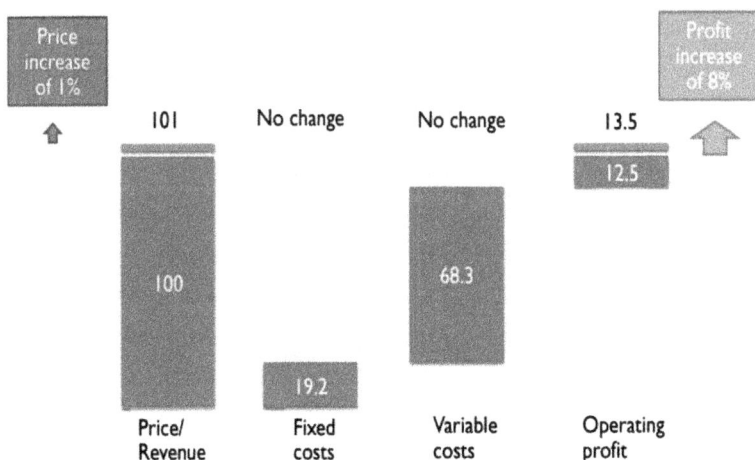

Figure 35

Philosophy at Play

Although pricing is a business-critical decision, few managers are skilled at pricing. This is hardly surprising given that pricing is a difficult decision involving complex interrelationships between price, margin, and volume. In the worst case, this can mean pricing is

- either abdicated to the sales department, in which case prices and profitability tend to be lower than they could otherwise be
- or to the accountants, in which case prices tend to be based on a cost-plus markup formula or the recovery of cost inflation

Neither situation is satisfactory because it results in a company failing to capture the true economic value of its products and services, and, consequently, the company underperforms.

When considering the pricing decision, it is critical to appreciate that customers buy benefits rather than products or services (i.e., a hole in the wall rather than a drill) and that they buy on value, not price per se.

Furthermore, not all customers are homogeneous. This means different customers will value the same product or service differently and are therefore prepared to pay different prices.

Whenever the customer value increases, a company will gain market share, and whenever the customer value diminishes, it will lose market share. In order to improve the value to the customer, a company can do one of two things. It can

- Add more benefits, although this may add cost
- Reduce its price, although this will reduce margin

Customers always buy the product or service they perceive to represent best value. The customer's perception of value is therefore always relative to the competition.

Adding more or new benefits to a product or service enables a company to increase its prices, providing these additional benefits are relevant and motivating to the target market customer. Adding benefits need not, however, necessarily lead to an increase in costs if value engineering is executed effectively.

There are five fundamental pricing relationships to understand:

- Demand relationship, i.e., how volume varies with changes in price
- Revenue relationship, i.e., how revenue varies with changes in price
- Cost relationship, i.e., how cost varies with volume and thus changes in price
- Profitability relationship, i.e., how revenue minus costs vary with changes in price
- Supply relationship, i.e., how volume supplied varies with changes in price

Unfortunately, in many companies, these relationships are rarely understood.

Price Range

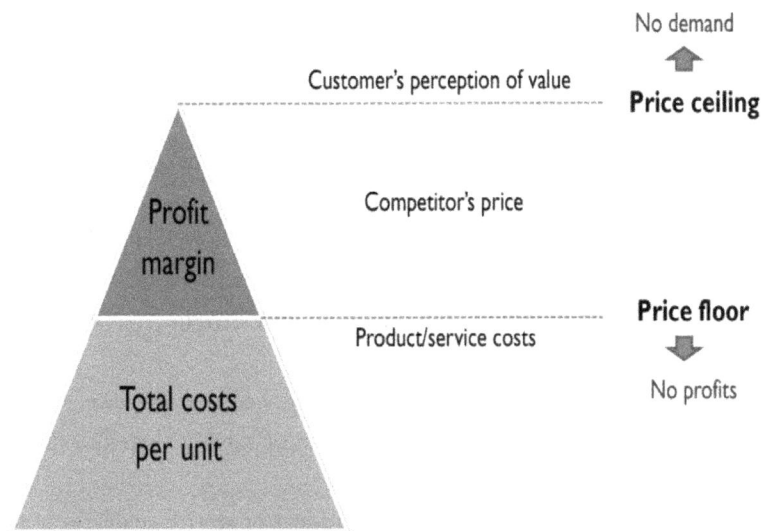

No demand

Customer's perception of value

Price ceiling

Profit margin

Competitor's price

Price floor

Product/service costs

No profits

Total costs per unit

Figure 36

Pricing Process

Companies use a product's price to achieve a variety of objectives. Simply put, the price of a product—the amount for which it's bought or sold—is an expression of the value of that product.

Of the four elements in the marketing mix—product, price, place, and promotion—price is the most flexible. A price can be changed relatively quickly. Price can also shape how consumers perceive a product. For example, think about sneakers—a high price might imply high quality, whereas a low price may imply the opposite. So there are potentially far-reaching implications. For this reason, different areas of an organization must have input on setting the "right" price. Sales, finance, operations, and marketing all have important roles to play.

Factors involved in setting the right price include production costs, consumer demand, competitors' price, and the product's value as perceived by consumers. However, at a deeper level, there's really only one primary consideration—what is the organization trying to achieve?

Areas that have the most input are finance and marketing. It's important to balance financial and marketing objectives and not to favor one area over another.

There are three primary financial objectives for pricing. One of these is to maximize the organization's return on investment, or ROI. Product development is very costly. An organization needs to recover these costs quickly, break even, and then quickly achieve the product's projected benefits. For example, a supplement that costs a lot to develop can be priced relatively high when it launches to recoup costs.

Another financial objective is to optimize profit. A balance has to be maintained between the short-term goal of making as much profit as possible and the long-term goal of retaining as many customers as possible.

A third financial objective is to increase cash flow. Organizations are always in need of cash to keep their operations going, and increased cash flow is a common objective.

Marketing's two primary objectives for a new product are to gain market share and maintain market stability. Market share is a key indicator of success; organizations sometimes decide to trade lower financial returns in exchange for increased market share. Maintaining market stability often means pricing a product in a way that doesn't rile competitors.

Going into the market aggressively with a low price, for example, could initiate a price war. Maintaining market stability, by comparison, enables an organization to establish its new product in the market and plan for the future.

The two areas of the organization that provide the most important input about price are finance and marketing. It's important to balance the objectives of these areas when determining your product's price.

Types of Strategies

There are a number of commonly used pricing strategies. These include the following:

Cost Plus

With cost plus, a markup is applied to the cost. Although easy to administer, cost plus is an ineffective way to price as it ignores the value to the customer and the impact on profitability resulting from changes in price, margin, and volume (Figure 37).

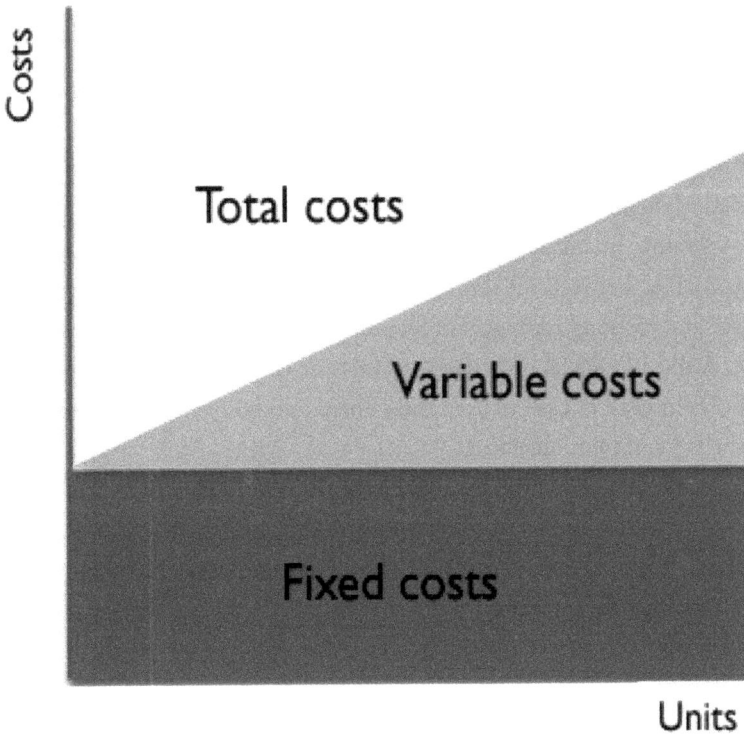

Figure 37

Price Taking

In markets where there are numerous small suppliers, the price is in effect set by the market forces of demand and supply, over which no individual supplier has any influence. Price taking is common in commodity markets with undifferentiated products or services.

Skimming

With price skimming, a company sets a high initial price during the early stage of a product's life cycle in order to capitalize on the product or service's novelty. As demand becomes more elastic owing to increased competition, prices are progressively lowered to retain competitiveness. This strategy is effective when there are high barriers to entry.

- Demand is price inelastic—i.e., large changes in price only have small effects on volume
- Product life cycles are short
- There is limited scope for economies of scale

With market skimming, an organization charges the highest possible price for its product. The rationale is that the product will have great value for a select group of consumers, and so they'll pay a high price for it.

Say you develop a new, innovative, and highly engaging product. It's unique in the market, and no one has anything like it anywhere. How would you price this marvel? It's quite likely that you'd charge the highest price that you think you can get.

Market skimming is an effective strategy when customers value a product very highly and consumers in the target market can afford the high price. Sometimes, it's also effective because special circumstances surrounding the use of a product justify a high price.

Penetration Pricing

With penetration pricing, a company sets a low initial price in order to capture a large share of the market quickly. This strategy is a long-term plan, in which losses may have to be accepted in the short term in order to discourage new entrants. Penetration pricing is an effective strategy when

A) There are low barriers to entry.
B) Demand is price elastic, i.e., small changes in price have large effects on volume.
C) There is mass market appeal for the product or service.
D) Product life cycles are long.
E) There is scope for economies of scale.

Market penetration, as a pricing strategy, is used when a low price may be the only way for a company to enter the market and differentiate its products from those of competitors. A low price can help a company penetrate a market and capture market share.

The market penetration strategy is sometimes used by companies to support the sale of other products. In this case, companies offer a product for sale at a price below cost price. Profit is made later by selling add-ons, services, or enhancements for the product—such as a laptop at a reduced price with the option of buying a webcam at an additional fee. The cheap or giveaway product is referred to as a "loss leader." So the product is sold at a loss, but it leads consumers to buy other, more profitable products.

You'd need to check with your legal department or company policies before using this strategy, because sometimes there are legal and ethical concerns to consider.

Market penetration is a good strategy when product differentiation isn't possible, a product can be offered at a low price in order to sell more expensive products, or a low price is needed to establish market presence or dominance.

Segmentation

With price segmentation, different prices are charged to different customers for essentially the same product or service. Price segmentation is widely practiced, and examples include peak versus off-peak travel and gym memberships. For segmentation to be an effective strategy,

A) The different segments must have different price elasticities
B) The lower price segment must not be able to resell to the higher price segment

Bundling

With bundling, a company prices a bundle of complementary goods and services at a price that is lower than the sum of the individual components, i.e., a packaged holiday or a Big Mac meal deal. Bundling is an effective strategy when

A) There is a low marginal cost of bundling
B) It captures an increased share of the available customer spend
C) It increases the customer's spend

Price Adaptation

An organization's pricing strategies are likely to fall into three categories—market skimming, market penetration, and price adaptation.

The third pricing strategy—price adaptation—is a hybrid of the market skimming and market penetration strategies. It involves setting different prices for different market segments. For example, a company may price its products differently in different regions or countries. Price adaptation is an effective strategy when the market can be segmented and targeted by pricing a product differently and discounts can be applied to move a product quickly.

Once pricing objectives are set, organizations develop the strategies that enable them to meet these objectives. The three main pricing strategies that organizations use are market skimming, market penetration, and price adaptation.

Understanding Your Product's Value to Customers

When it comes to setting prices, there are a variety of strategies, but one factor is key: value to the customer. The most common methods for pricing are flawed because they ignore this essential aspect.

For instance, *cost-plus pricing* works by taking costs and adding a percentage to arrive at the selling price. However, this means that in reality there's no connection between what it costs to produce something and what it sells for.

So suppose it costs $15 to make something that you sell for $20. You find a way to reduce your costs to $13 and therefore decrease your selling price to $18. The issue with this approach is that your customers still value the product at $20, which they've been willing to pay hitherto.

Another equally flawed approach is to *price below your competitors*. The problem with this strategy is that you can't know how much value consumers place on your competitors' products. It could be that they value your goods more and are willing to pay a price that reflects that. Hence, both these strategies miss the point, which is value to the customer.

A better strategy is to base pricing on what a product is worth to consumers. That's because customers don't ask themselves what a product costs to make; they ask how much value it brings to them. So when setting a price, you have to consider the added value of your product and how it makes the lives of your customers easier.

Suppose you're selling a hair dryer that costs a little more than most of the others on the market but comes with a 5-year guarantee. Although the hair dryer might cost the same to make as a less costly one, your long-term guarantee is an added value and will be perceived as such by customers, so you can charge more than the competition.

But this raises a bigger question: how exactly does value work?

Relationship of Price to Value

How do you choose which TV to buy when you're overwhelmed by the selection at your local electronics store? Well, most people make purchase decisions based on how much they value any given product.

For instance, take a quality pair of headphones that sell for $100. If you value them at $100 because of your affinity to the brand, you will consider the price fair. If you valued the same headphones at $130, you'd consider $100 a bargain, and if you valued them at $70 you probably wouldn't buy them, opting instead for a cheaper model or one with features you value more.

So to be able to charge a given price, you first have to make sure your customers know why your product is valuable. One way to do this is by talking to customers about it. You can simply give them a price range and discuss the different options.

For instance, if you offer a service like hairdressing, you might give customers a price range between $50 and $150 depending on different options. By showing your customers the costs of extras, you communicate the added value of these options.

That means a basic haircut could cost $50, but additional hair care and styling would run closer to $120. Given these options, your client wills choose what they're willing to pay for according to the value they place on different services.

CHAPTER 7

Investment Appraisal

Time Value of Money

So what does discounting cash flows (DCF) entail? Why do we consider it to be the gold standard in finance?

We start with a simple example.

I've got two propositions for you; which one would you prefer?

A) I either give you $100 now, or
B) I promise to give you $100 in a year's time.

Which one do you prefer?

It wouldn't be surprising if you said that you very much preferred the $100 right now.

And that is indeed what most people would intuitively reply. They prefer money in hand rather than to wait for the same amount of money at some point in the future.

But why is that?

Why is the $100 today somehow valued differently from $100 in the future?

Well, we have at least three good reasons why you might prefer the $100 right now

A) We've seen over many, many years that dollars over time reduce in value owing to price increases. Inflation erodes the value of money over time. So what you can buy with $100 today is going to be worth probably more than what you can buy with the $100 in a year's time.

B) The second reason why you might prefer the $100 now is that you might not get it. I might walk away, and you'll end up empty-handed in 1 year's time. You are faced with a risk: Will the cash flow actually occur? If you get the money now, there is no risk. But 1 year from today, who knows what can happen in that time period.

C) And lastly, opportunity costs.

The key point is that we cannot directly compare dollars, cash flows that occur at different points in time. We need to consider the actual date that a cash flow eventuates. So we need to consider the value of those cash flows at different points in time, somehow accounting for expected inflation, for risk, and for opportunity costs, alternative investment opportunities for investors. The way we do that is as follows: We account for what we labeled the time value of money, how a dollar changes in value from one-time period to the next time period by systematically discounting future cash flows.

Let's take a closer look (Figure 38).

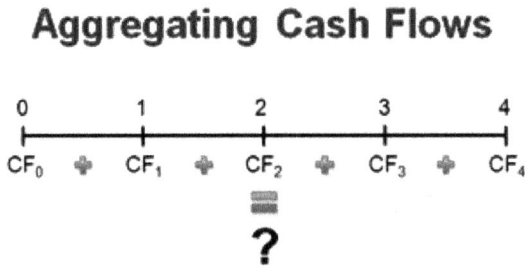

Figure 38

Can we add/subtract cash flows in different time periods?

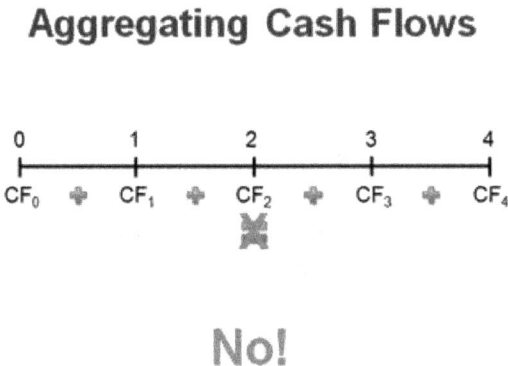

Figure 39

Aggregating Cash Flows

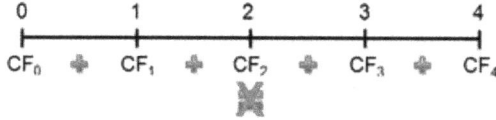

Lesson: Never* add/subtract cash
flows received at different times

Figure 40

Never add/subtract cash flows from different time periods
Use (i.e., multiply by) discount factor to change cash flows' time units
$(1+R)^t$

A) $t < 0$ moves CF back in time (discounting)
B) $t > 0$ moves CF forward in time (compounding)

DCF moves them to a common point.

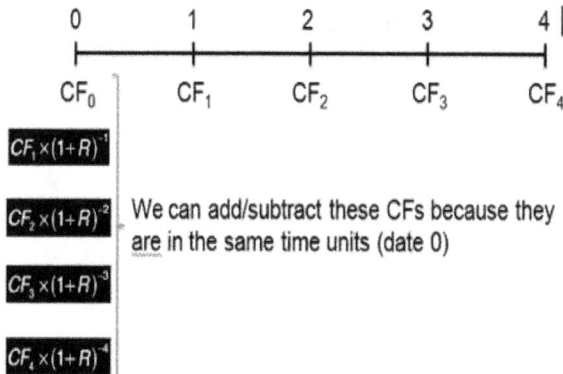

Figure 41

Understand the Cost of Capital

Cost of capital is the cost of the funds used to finance a business. It depends on the method of financing used. Most companies use a combination of debt (such as short-term notes or long-term bonds) and equity to finance their businesses. Such companies often derive their overall cost of capital from a weighted average of all capital sources. This is called the weighted average cost of capital (WACC), because each type of capital (common stock, preferred stock, bonds, other long-term debt) is weighted according to its proportion in the company's capital structure. WACC is determined by the external market, not the company.

When investors give their money to a company, they expect to receive a return by way of compensation. For lenders, compensation is in the form of interest, and for shareholders, it is in the form of dividends and share price appreciation. The minimum rate of return required by investors is called the "opportunity cost of capital," which represents the rate of return foregone by not investing in an alternative investment with the same level of risk. The WACC for a company is the opportunity cost of capital for each investor type (i.e., lenders and shareholders) weighted by the amount of funds provided by each investor type. The WACC represents the minimum return on investment required to create value.

The WACC represents a "hurdle rate," or minimum acceptable return rate, that the company would have to earn before the investment generates value. So it is extensively used in the capital budgeting process to determine whether the company should proceed with an investment.

Money that the firm has today is more valuable than future payments because current money can be invested to earn money (Figure 42).

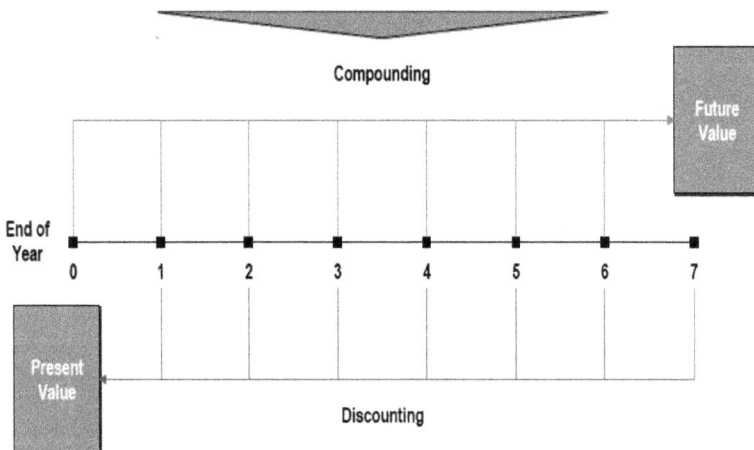

Figure 42

One of the most important decisions for any business is investment, of which there are two general types:

A) Investment for growth, i.e., increased capacity, new products and services, marketing expenditure, etc.
B) Investment for efficiency, i.e., investments that reduce costs and/or improve productivity

When considering an investment decision, a company will undertake an investment appraisal that will consider:

A) The size or cost of the investment
B) The internal return on investment
C) The payback period
D) The risk associated with the investment (Figure 43)

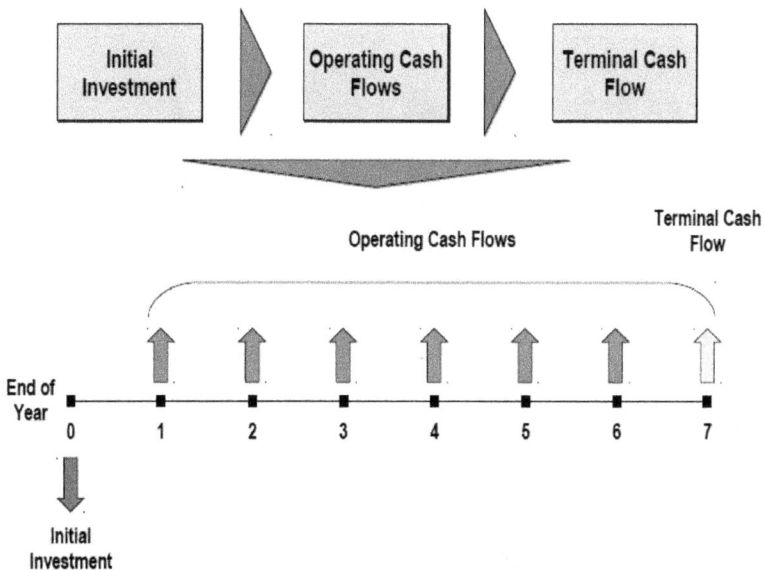

Figure 43

Most companies start by estimating the impact of the investment on current and future cash flows and compare them with investment situation to a without investment base case.

The general rule is that we are interested in all future, incremental (or extra) cash flows to the company as a result of undertaking the investment. We are not interested in the following:

A) money already committed (or sunk costs)
B) historic costs noncash flows (especially depreciation)
C) book values ⊙ interest costs (because these are dealt with by the discounting)

We are interested in both direct and opportunity cash costs and revenues. Direct costs are those costs directly related to the investment; e.g., the new machine will incur running costs of $10,000 per year. Opportunity costs are costs that occur elsewhere in the company owing to acceptance of an investment; e.g., buying a new machine will result in losing revenue of $10,000 per year that is currently being earned by the company from another machine.

Types of Techniques

Organizations may use any one or more capital investment evaluation techniques (Figure 44)

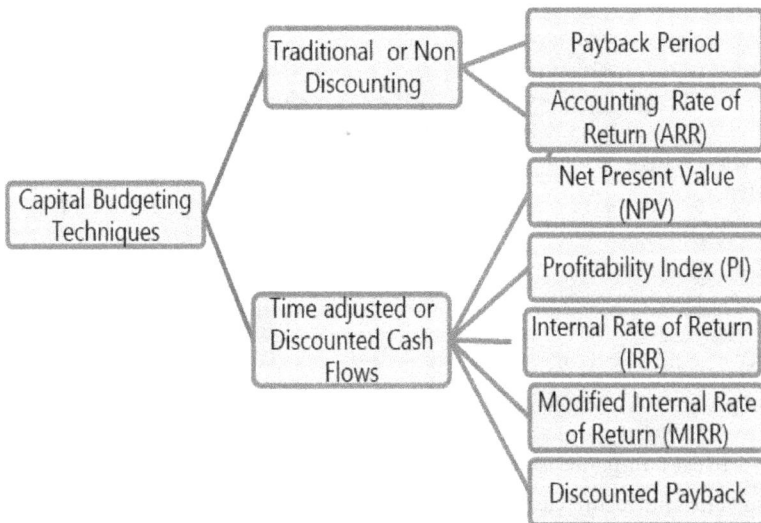

Figure 44

Payback Period

Payback on an investment is the period of time (projected or actual) that it takes for the incremental discounted cash flows associated with the investment to pay back the initial capital investment.

The payback period is useful when the future flows have a high level of uncertainty. The further into the future we are forecasting, the more uncertain the flows are likely to be. By choosing projects with faster payback periods, we are more certain that the projects will indeed end up making a surplus (Figure 45).

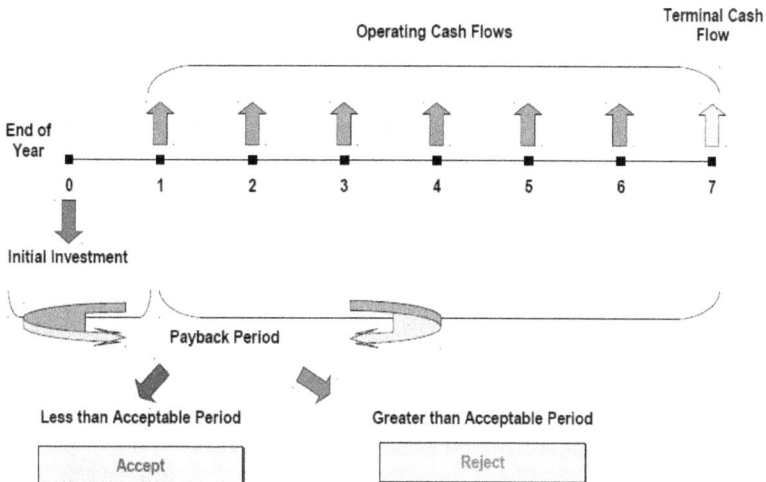

Figure 45

If the initial investment were $10m, and payback achieved in year 3, more than $10m of incremental cash would need to be generated from the investment in order to achieve payback. This is because cash today is worth less than the same amount of cash yesterday and more than the same amount of cash tomorrow.

Accounting (Book) Rate of Return (ARR) or Average Rate of Return (ARR)

The accounting rate of return of an investment measures the average annual net income of the project (incremental income) as a percentage of the investment.

Accounting rate of return = Average annual net income/Investment

The numerator is the average annual net income generated by the project over its useful life. The denominator can be either the initial investment (including installation cost) or the average investment over the useful life of the project

Net Present Value (NPV)/Internal Rate of Return (IRR)

The incremental cash flows associated with the investment (i.e., the cash flows over and above the base case) are discounted by the company's average weighted cost of capital (WACC) to produce a single figure that values the cash flows in today's money. This is called the NPV of the investment.

If the NPV is positive, the project will yield a return greater than the company's WACC and will therefore create value, whereas if the NPV is negative, the investment would yield less than WACC and thereby destroy value.

IRR is the interest rate at which the NPV of all the cash flows (both positive and negative) from a project or investment equal zero. If the IRR of a new project exceeds a company's required rate of return, that project is desirable.

As with any set of estimates, garbage in generates garbage out. Consequently, any robust investment appraisal will also assess the impact of changes in assumptions on the projected cash flows and thus the NPV associated with the investment. This is called sensitivity analysis.

In addition, a company will also calculate the IRR and payback period associated with the investment. The internal rate of return is the discount rate that would result in a zero NPV; the higher the IRR, the more attractive the investment.

Most companies are often confronted with a choice of investment projects and only limited funds available. In such circumstances, the company has to choose between competing projects. Over and above conducting an investment appraisal on each individual project, a company can also compare the NPV of each project per $1m invested. The resulting measure is helpful for assessing which value-creating investment (i.e., those with an NPV greater than zero or an IRR greater than the WACC) is the most efficient (Figures 46 and 47).

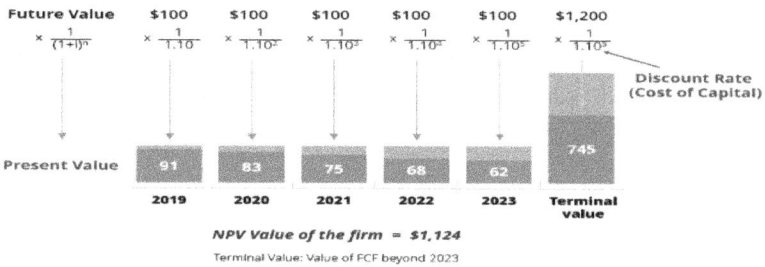

Figure 46

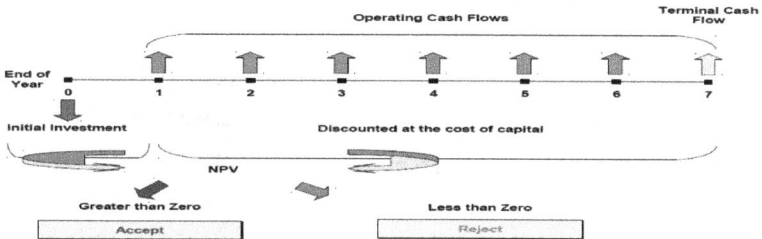

Figure 47

Other Considerations

The amount of capital invested is also a measure of risk, and thus a company may prefer a portfolio of several lower yielding, "less risky" investment projects than one more attractive, "higher risk" big roll of the dice. Efficiency investments are generally considered to be lower risk than growth investments. This is because there are more knowns with the former, and, consequently, future cash flow projections should be more robust. Nevertheless, empirical studies show that growth investments have a much greater effect on creating value than efficiency investments.

Furthermore, when considering investment decisions, it is also important to remember that not all investments are capitalized on the balance sheet. For example, investments in

A) Sales and marketing activities
B) Training and development
C) Research and development

are usually charged to the profit and loss account rather than capitalized on the balance sheet. This is because most accountants consider these costs to be margin reducing expenses rather than investments per se. Nevertheless, irrespective of the accounting treatment, an investment is an investment and cash is cash. All investments of cash need rigorous appraisal, not just those capitalized on the balance sheet by the accountants.

Creating and Destroying Value

In economics, the value of a company is known as its enterprise value and is the NPV of the company's future free cash flows discounted by its weighted average opportunity cost of capital WACC. Value is said to be created whenever a company's enterprise value increases and is said to be destroyed whenever the enterprise value of the company decreases. Investments with a positive NPV, or an IRR greater than a company's WACC, create value, whereas investments with a negative NPV, or an IRR less than a company's WACC, destroy value.

It is, however, incorrect to conclude that a company that increases its profit in any given year has created value or that a company where profitability has decreased has destroyed value. This is because profit in any given year is a single period measure, whereas the enterprise value of a company is determined by its future free cash flow performance. Indeed, a company that increases its profitability in 1 year may in fact be destroying value. Such a situation could arise if the company were either making insufficient investments to retain its competitiveness or has made a misguided value-destroying investment decision. Similarly, a company where profitability decreased in any given year may be creating value by improving its ability to compete or because it has made a number of value-creating investment decisions whose financial benefits have yet to materialize in the current year's profit and loss account

Illustration

Alpha Company is considering the following investment projects

| Projects | Cash Flows (₹) | | | |
	C_0	C_1	C_2	C_3
A	−10,000	+10,000		
B	−10,000	+7,500	+7,500	
C	−10,000	+2,000	+4,000	+12,000
D	−10,000	+10,000	+3,000	+3,000

A) *Analyze* and rank the projects according to each of the following methods:

(i) Payback, (ii) ARR, (iii) IRR, and (iv) NPV, assuming discount rates of 10 and 30 percent.

B) Assuming the projects are independent, which one should be accepted? If the projects are mutually exclusive, *identify* which project is the best?

Solution

(a) (i) Payback Period

Project A: 10,000/10,000 = 1 year

Project B: 10,000/7,500 = 1 1/3 years.

Project C: 2 years + (10,000 − 6,000)/12,000 = 2 1/3 years

Project D: 1 year.

(ii) ARR

Project A :(10,000 − 10,000)1/2/(10,000)1/2 = 0

Project B: (15,000 − 10,000)1/2/(10,000)1/2 = 2,500/5,000 = 50%

Project C: (18,000 − 10,000)1/3/(10,000)1/2 = 2,667/5,000= 53%

Project D: (16,000 − 10,000)1/3/(10,000)1/2 = 2,000/5,000 = 40%

Note: This net cash proceed includes recovery of investment also. Therefore, net cash earnings are found by deducting initial investment.

(iii) IRR

Project A:	The net cash proceeds in year 1 are just equal to investment. Therefore, r = 0%.
Project B:	This project produces an annuity of 7,500 for 2 years. Therefore, the required Present Value Annuity Factor (PVAF)is 10,000/7,500 = 1.33. This factor is found under the 32% column. Therefore, r = 32%.
Project C:	Since cash flows are uneven, the trial and error method will be followed. At a 20% rate of discount, the NPV is + 1,389. At 30% rate of discount, the NPV is −633. The true rate of return should be less than 30%. At a 27% rate of discount, it is found that the NPV is −86, and at 26% +105. Through interpolation, we find r = 26.5%.
Project D:	In this case also, by using the trial and error method it is found that at a 37.6% rate of discount NPV becomes almost zero. Therefore, r = 37.6%.

(iv) NPV

Project A:

at 10%: $-10,000 + 10,000 \times 0.909 = -910$

at 30%: $-10,000 + 10,000 \times 0.769 = -2,310$

Project B:

at 10% : $-10,000 + 7,500(0.909 + 0.826) = 3,013$

at 30%: $-10,000 + 7,500(0.769 + 0.592) = +208$

Project C:

at 10%: $-10,000 + 2,000 \times 0.909 + 4,000 \times 0.826 + 12,000 \times 0.751 = +4,134$

at 30%: $-10,000 + 2,000 \times 0.769 + 4,000 \times 0.592 + 12,000 \times 0.455 = -633$

Project D:

at 10%: $-10,000 + 10,000 \times 0.909 + 3,000 \times (0.826 + 0.751) = +3,821$

at 30%: $-10,000 + 10,000 \times 0.769 + 3,000 \times (0.592 + 0.455) = +831$

The projects are ranked as follows according to the various methods

Ranks					
Projects	PBP	ARR	IRR	NPV (10%)	NPV (30%)
A	1	4	4	4	4
B	2	2	2	3	2
C	3	1	3	1	3
D	1	3	1	2	1

c) Payback and ARR are a theoretically unsound method for choosing between the investment projects. Between the two time-adjusted Discounted Cash Flow (DCF) investment criteria, NPV and IRR, NPV gives consistent results. If the projects are independent (and there is no capital rationing), either IRR or NPV can be used because the same set of projects will be accepted by either of the methods. In the present case, except Project A, all the three projects should be accepted if the discount rate is 10 percent. Only Projects B and D should be undertaken if the discount rate is 30 percent.

If it is assumed that the projects are mutually exclusive, then under the assumption of a 30 percent discount rate, the choice is between B and D (A and C are unprofitable). Both criteria IRR and NPV give the same results—D is the best. Under the assumption of a 10 percent discount rate, ranking according to IRR and NPV conflict (except for Project A). If the IRR rule is followed, Project D should be accepted. But by the NPV rule, Project C is the best. The NPV rule generally gives consistent results in conformity with the wealth maximization principle. Therefore, Project C should be accepted following the NPV rule.

Investment Appraisal

The investment decision: Decisions have to be made as to where capital is to be invested. For example, is it worth launching a new product? Is it worth expanding the factory? Is it worth acquiring another company? It is the financial manager's role to decide which criteria to employ in making this kind of investment decision (Figure 48).

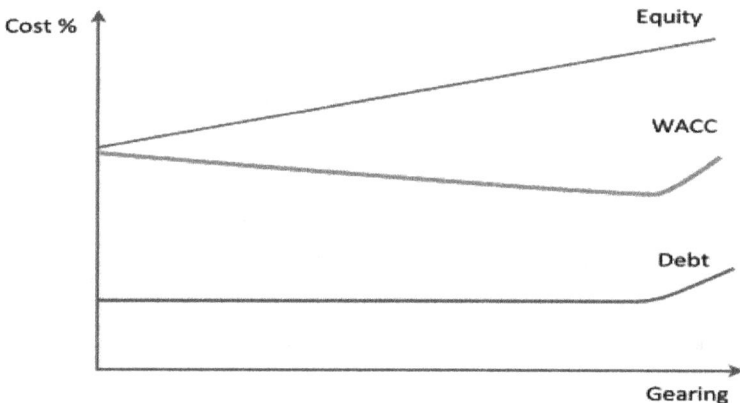

Figure 48

Capital Asset Pricing Model (CAPM)

Shares in some companies are viewed as inherently more risky than shares in other companies because the nature of their business is more risky. As a result, the potential fluctuations in profits (and hence dividends) in the future are greater. If things go well, shareholders may well receive much higher dividends, but the risk is that things may go badly, in which case they will receive much lower dividends. The greater the potential fluctuations in returns, the greater we say that the risk is. There are two different reasons why one company may be more risky than another:

A) Unsystematic risk (or company-specific risk)
   This is risk due to factors within the particular company, such as poor labor relations or the appointment of a new management director.

B) Systematic risk (or market risk)
   This is risk due to general economic factors, such as the level of inflation or changes in the exchange rate. A shareholder can "remove" the unsystematic risk by creating a portfolio of shares on the basis that although each share individually has unsystematic risk, it "cancels out" with the risk of other shares in the portfolio. We say that a well-diversified portfolio is one where the unsystematic risk has been completely removed (i.e., diversified away).

Systematic risk exists in all companies and cannot be removed—all companies will be affected by, for example, the level of inflation. However, the level of systematic risk depends on the type of business and will be different for different types of business. Although each individual shareholder may not hold a well-diversified portfolio of shares, we assume that shareholders overall are well diversified.

There are several ways in which we could attempt to measure the systematic risk of an investment, but the standard way is to measure it relative to the risk of the stock exchange as a whole. The stock exchange index is the average of all the shares on the stock exchange and is risky (in that it fluctuates). Some shares fluctuate more than the average, whereas some fluctuate less than the average.

We use β to measure the systematic risk, and β is defined as the systematic risk of the investment as a proportion of the risk of the market (or stock exchange) as a whole. CAPM therefore assumes that it is the level of systematic risk that determines the required return from an investment.

- If an investment has a β of 1, it has 1 times the risk of the market; i.e., it has the same risk as the market.
- If an investment has a $\beta > 1$, then it is more risky than the market.

- If an investment has a $\beta < 1$, then it is less risky than the market.
- If an investment has a β of 0, then it has zero risk, or we say that it is risk free.

If the financial manager is considering an investment in a new project, then because it is shareholders' money that is being invested, the investment should be appraised in the same way as would be done by shareholders if they were investing their money directly.

As a result, the required return from the project (and hence the discount rate) should be calculated from the β of the project.

Capital Rationing

Capital rationing is the term used to cover the situation when the company has limited funds available for investment. This can be either because there is only a limited amount available to be borrowed (hard capital rationing) or, alternatively, the company decides to itself place a limit on the amount that it is prepared to borrow (soft capital rationing). The object of the exercise is to decide how best to invest a limited amount of capital available when there are several investments available. The best solution will be the one giving the greatest total NPV. The approach to be used depends on whether or not the projects are infinitely divisible.

The approach is as follows:

A) calculate the NPV per $ of initial investment (the profitability index)
B) rank the projects in terms of their profitability indexes
C) invest as much as possible in the project with the highest profitability index, then go to the project with the next highest, and so on until the capital available is exhausted.

Illustration

Shiva Limited is planning its capital investment program for next year. It has five projects, all of which give a positive NPV at the company cutoff rate of 15 percent, the investment outflows and present values being as follows:

Project	Investment	NPV @ 15%
	₹000	₹000
A	(50)	15.4
B	(40)	18.7
C	(25)	10.1
D	(30)	11.2
E	(35)	19.3

The company is limited to a capital spending of 1,20,000.

You are required to *illustrate* the returns from a package of projects within the capital spending limit. The projects are independent of each other and are divisible (i.e., part-project is possible).

Computation of NPVs per Rs 1 of investment and ranking of the projects

Project	Investment	NPV @ 15%	NPV per ₹1 invested	Ranking
	₹'000	₹'000		
A	(50)	15.4	0.31	5
B	(40)	18.7	0.47	2
C	(25)	10.1	0.40	3
D	(30)	11.2	0.37	4
E	(35)	19.3	0.55	1

Building up of a Program of Projects Based on Their Rankings

Project	Investment	NPV @ 15%
	₹000	₹000
E	(35)	19.3
B	(40)	18.7
C	(25)	10.1
D	(20)	7.5
	120	55.6

(2/3 of project total)

Thus, Project A should be rejected and only two-thirds of Project D undertaken. If the projects are not divisible, then other combinations can be examined as follows:

	Investment	NPV @ 15%
	₹ 000	₹000
E + B + C	100	48.1
E + B + D	105	49.2

In this case, E + B + D would be preferable because it provides a higher NPV despite D ranking lower than C.

Lease versus Buy

When deciding whether or not an investment is worthwhile, we usually assume that we will be purchasing the asset. However, having made the acquisition decision, we could be required to consider financing the machine by way of leasing it rather than by outright purchase. In order to make this financing decision, we need to calculate the Present Value (PV) of the costs of buying the assets with the PV of the costs of leasing the asset. In both cases, we will discount at the after-tax cost of borrowing and choose that method that gives the lower PV (and hence least cost).

After-Tax Cash Flows of Lease

Periodic after-tax cash flows of lease = (maintenance costs + lease rentals) × (1 − tax rate)

Terminal after-tax cash flows = periodic after-tax cash flows + amount paid to purchase the asset

After-Tax Cash Flows of Purchase

The most significant component of cash outflows if the asset is purchased is the payment for the cost of the asset. If the company uses its own funds, the total cost is assumed to be paid at the time 0; however, if the company obtains a loan to finance the purchase, the loan repayment and associated tax shield on interest shall appear in all the periods of the lease analysis.

Other cash flows include the tax shield on depreciation, any potential savings, maintenance costs, insurance, etc., associated with the purchase and use of the asset.

About the Author

Anurag Singal is a chartered accountant and an MBA from IIM Ahmedabad. He ranked 22nd and 25th all-India in CA Final and CA PE-II, respectively. He received the "CA Professional Achiever-Manufacturing Sector" award at the 6th ICAI Awards in February 2013 for his professional accomplishments in leading corporate houses across India.

Mr. Singal has mentored hundreds of young chartered accountants, and his articles on a range of contemporary topics have been published in various journals.

He is a visiting faculty for Corporate Finance at various B-schools in India; he also has a popular YouTube channel on career guidance and financial planning.

He is the chief mentor of cajobportal.com, India's first job portal exclusively for chartered accountants.

Mr. Singal has authored books such as *Accounting for People Who Think They Hate Accounting*, *The Art and Science of Financial Modeling*, *MS Excel—Let's advance to the next level*, published by Business Expert Press, USA.

Index

OTHER TITLES FROM THE FINANCE AND FINANCIAL MANAGEMENT COLLECTION

John Doukas, *Editor*

- *Blockchain Hurricane: Origins, Applications, and Future of Blockchain and Cryptocurrency* by Kate Baucherel
- *Risk Management for Nonprofit Organizations* by Rick Nason and Omer Livvarcin
- *Conservative Options Trading: Hedging Strategies, Cash Cows, and Loss Recovery* by Michael C. Thomsett
- *Understanding Behavioral BIA$: A Guide to Improving Financial Decision-Making Business* by Daniel C. Krawczyk and George H. Baxter
- *Understanding Momentum in Investment Technical Analysis: Making Better Predictions Based on Price, Trend Strength, and Speed of Change* by Michael C. Thomsett
- *Valuation of Indian Life Insurance Companies* by Prasanna Rajesh
- *Escape from the Central Bank Trap, Second Edition: How to Escape From the $20 Trillion Monetary Expansion Unharmed* by Daniel Lacalle
- *Trade Credit and Risk Management* by Lucia Gibilaro
- *The Art and Science of Financial Modeling* by Anurag Singal
- *Trade Credit and Financing Instruments* by Lucia Gibilaro
- *Understanding Cryptocurrencies: The Money of the Future* by Arvind Matharu
- *Risk and Win! A Simple Guide to Managing Risks in Small and Medium-Sized Organizations* by John Harvey Murray
- *Welcome to My Trading Room, Volume III: Basics to Trading Global Shares, Futures, and Forex–Advanced Methodologies and Strategies* by Jacques Magliolo
- *Applied International Finance Volume I, Second Edition: Managing Foreign Exchange Risk* by Thomas J. O'Brien
- *Global Mergers and Acquisitions, Second Edition: Combining Companies Across Borders, Volume I* by Abdol S. Soofi and Yuqin Zhang
- *Global Mergers and Acquisitions, Second Edition: Combining Companies Across Borders, Volume II* by Abdol S. Soofi and Yuqin Zhang

Announcing the Business Expert Press Digital Library

Concise e-books business students need for classroom and research

This book can also be purchased in an e-book collection by your library as

- *a one-time purchase,*
- *that is owned forever,*
- *allows for simultaneous readers,*
- *has no restrictions on printing, and*
- *can be downloaded as PDFs from within the library community.*

Our digital library collections are a great solution to beat the rising cost of textbooks. E-books can be loaded into their course management systems or onto students' e-book readers.
The **Business Expert Press** digital libraries are very affordable, with no obligation to buy in future years. For more information, please visit **www.businessexpertpress.com/librarians**.
To set up a trial in the United States, please email **sales@businessexpertpress.com**.